ANNOUNCING

2 NEW Streamliners

CHICAGO NORTH WESTERN LINE
UNION PACIFIC OVERLAND ROUTE

CITY OF LOS ANGELES
and
CITY OF SAN FRANCISCO

THE ART OF THE
STREAMLINER

BOB JOHNSTON AND JOE WELSH
WITH MIKE SCHAFER

MetroBooks

ACKNOWLEDGMENTS

The authors and producers of this book extend their appreciation to all those who provided assistance and other support in this book project. In particular we would like to thank artist and designer Mitch Markovitz for the seven special illustrations of car interiors that he did expressly for *The Art of the Streamliner*. Few people we know have quite the understanding of industrial design—especially as it relates to the passenger train—than Mitch, who aside from doing wonderful fine-art paintings has designed locomotive paint schemes, railroad passenger timetables, crew uniforms, and travel posters for various railroads.

We also extend a hearty thanks to William F. Howes Jr. for his assistance in providing illustration and information pertaining to matters of the Baltimore & Ohio Railroad, whose passenger department he headed in the 1960s.

Many thanks go to fellow passenger-train aficionado Kevin J. Holland for the loan of several photos, train brochures, and folders for the project. Similarly, we appreciate the generosity of James A. Neubauer for his wide array of vintage streamliner photography.

The folks at the Union Pacific Museum in Omaha, Nebraska, in particular William Kratville, were especially prompt and helpful in providing us with many of the quality UP and Southern Pacific photos that appear within these pages.

Thanks must also go to Jim Boyd, formerly the editor of *Railfan & Railroad* magazine for his help in providing illustrative material and—with his insight as a former Electro-Motive employee—the fascinating sidebar, "Styling the Streamliners," that appears in chapter 4. Likewise, we thank Kevin P. Keefe, past editor and associate publisher of *Trains* Magazine and longtime friend, for providing an entertaining foreword.

Applause is also in order for Cesar Vergara, formerly of Amtrak's group, for helping prove that passenger-train styling is not a lost art.

In closing, we also extend our appreciation to the following people, institutions, and companies: Alan L. Bradley, Burdell Bulgrin, Chris Burger, the California State Railroad Museum, Al Chione, William T. Clynes, John Dziobko, the Hagley Museum and Library, Herbert H. Harwood, Jim Heuer, Gerald Hook, Oliver "Dee" Joseph/Private Car Limited, Mike McBride, John Forbes McClean, the Milwaukee Road Historical Association, Jonathan Nelson, David P. Oroszi, Dave Randall/RPC Publications, Howard Robbins, G. William Schafer III, Robert P. Schmidt, Alvin Schultze, Jim Shaughnessy, Steve Smedley, Jay Williams, and Robert Yanosey/Morning Sun Books.

—Bob Johnston
—Joe Welsh
—Mike Schafer
November 2000

FRONT COVER: UNION PACIFIC MUSEUM COLLECTION

FRONTISPIECE: A colorful brochure for Union Pacific's new *City of San Francisco* and *City of Los Angeles* streamliners of 1937 serves as a reminder that the streamlined train was a silver lining of the Great Depression. JOE WELSH COLLECTION

TITLE PAGE: One of the greatest passenger trains ever to roll, New York Central's 1938-edition *20th Century Limited* races through Garrison, New York, on the morning of June 24, 1939, en route from Chicago to Grand Central Terminal in Manhattan. CHRIS BURGER COLLECTION

CONTENTS PAGE: The lounge observation car of the Atlantic Coast Line-Florida East Coast *Champion* streamliner of 1939 sweeps through an idyllic Florida beach scene in a painting by railroad-theme artist Leslie Ragan. JOE WELSH COLLECTION

MetroBooks

An Imprint of Friedman/Fairfax Publishers

First published in 2001 by MetroBooks, 122 Fifth Ave, New York, NY 10011

Library of Congress Cataloging-in-Publication Data available upon request.

ISBN 1-58663-146-2

Editing, design, and pre-production by Mike Schafer, Andover Junction Publications, Lee, Illinois, and Blairstown, New Jersey.
Color separations by Leefung-Asco Printers Ltd.
Printed in China by Leefung-Asco Printers Ltd.

10 9 8 7 6 5 4 3 2 1

For bulk purchases and special sales, please contact:
Friedman/Fairfax Publishers
Attention: Sales Department
15 West 26th Street
New York, NY 10010
212/685-6610   FAX 212/685-1307

Visit our website:
www.metrobooks.com

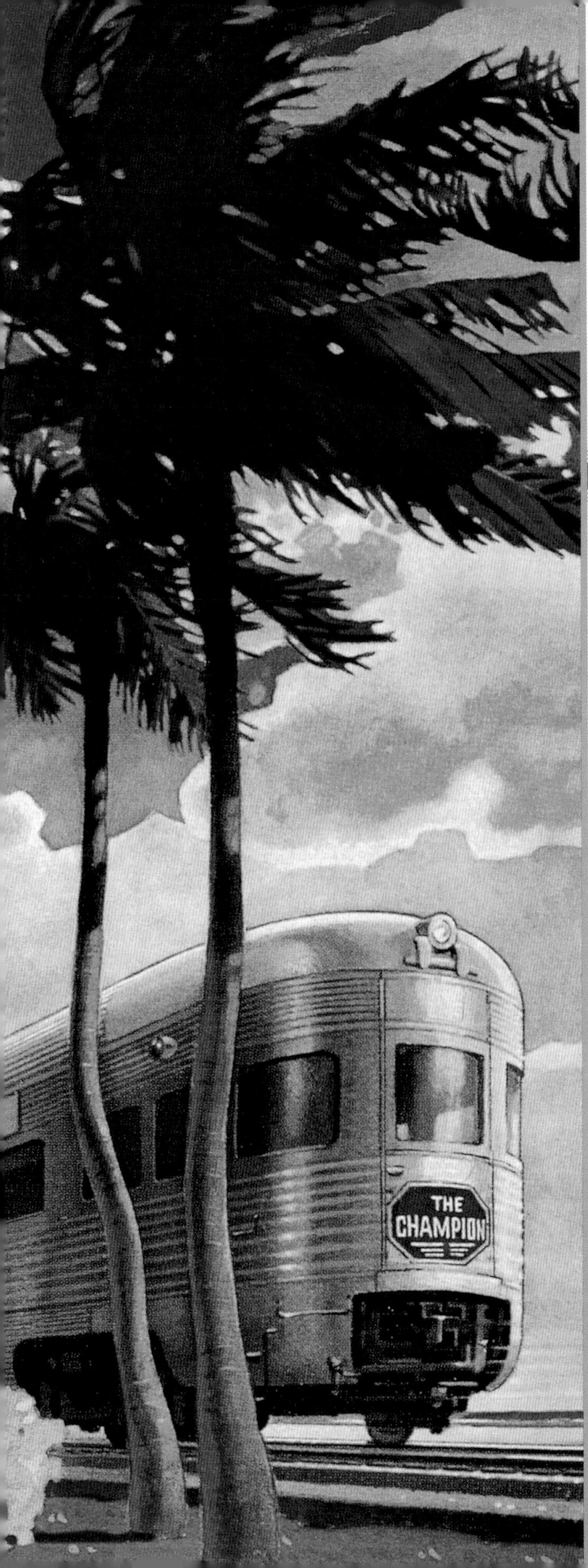

THE ART OF THE STREAMLINER

CONTENTS

FOREWORD

Passengers on the station platforms at Savanna, Illinois, on September 15, 1938, admire their sleek conveyance—the *Morning Zephyr*, 1936 edition—as it pulls in from Minneapolis. Once passengers are all aboard, the *Zephyr* will make quick work of the 145 miles across northern Illinois to Chicago. J.M. GRUBER COLLECTION

I magine you're a railroad passenger, standing on a crowded station platform on an evening in 1935. You're a regular on this railroad, which means the train you're about to board hasn't changed much since the turn of the century. It will roll into town behind a noisy, black, smoking steam locomotive. Trailing the engine will be a long line of cars distinguished mainly by dark paint, small windows, and rivets. When the train rolls to a stop, you'll climb aboard into a world of dim light, muted colors, and rough old plush upholstery.

But wait! Something's different about this train. Through the glare of the approaching headlight you can see that there's no smoke, no bark of a steamer's exhaust. Your eyes catch a momentary glint of silver, then, finally, a sight for sore eyes: a sleek, stainless-steel, diesel-powered train of the future. Surprise! The *Zephyr* has arrived.

This scene can only be imagined, but versions of it must have occurred every time the Burlington Route's flashy new *Zephyr* trains entered service across the Midwest in the mid- to late-1930s. In fact, it's something that happened all across America through the mid-1950s as the traveling public fell under the spell of the streamliner. It was a time when railroads fought each other tooth and nail for the travel market, going into battle with a whole generation of trains known for their bold technology and high style.

The technology made everything possible, but it was the style that captured the public's fancy. One by one, nearly all the major railroads entered the streamliner sweepstakes, each going to great lengths to establish carefully crafted brand identities. The New York Central's *20th Century Limited* of 1938 was an Art Deco fantasy with the food and service to match. The Milwaukee Road's *Hiawatha*s were speed demons seen in a blur of orange and maroon. The Santa Fe's *Super Chief* took an old name and made it sexy with a fast Chicago–L.A. schedule and gourmet food in the Turquoise Room. And three railroads—Burlington, Rio Grande, and Western Pacific—teamed up to create the *California Zephyr*, the trailblazing cruise train that made dome cars synonymous with scenery.

In a word, the passenger-train business was "hot." Today's airlines wage war for the domestic business traveler and the trans-oceanic tourist. But these battles are no more spirited—nor fascinating—than the titanic struggles of the streamliner era. In those days, New York Central worked hard to beat archrival Pennsylvania Railroad for the New York-Chicago market, and the Pennsy gave as good as it got. Long before their merger, the Atlantic Coast Line and the Seaboard tried every trick in the book to gain an edge in the Florida trade. And for a time, Burlington Route, Milwaukee Road, and the Chicago & North Western fought a three-way grudge match in the Chicago-Twin Cities corridor. The winner: lucky travelers who enjoyed a range of choices as rich as any available today at O'Hare, Kennedy, or LAX.

Authors Bob Johnston and Joe Welsh and *The Art of the Streamliner* editor and designer and writer Mike Schafer have captured the excitement of those heady days in this fascinating history. All three have strong credentials as passenger-train journalists and historians. And all three know the joy and satisfaction of train travel as represented by the fabulous trains in this book. Take a ride through these pages and you'll gladly surrender to the mystical call of "All Aboard!"

Kevin P. Keefe, Editor
Trains Magazine
Waukesha, Wisconsin
April 2000

INTRODUCTION

In a sense, this book is a tribute to architects and designers all over the world—regardless of whether they're orchestrating the look and charisma of New York's Chrysler Building, San Francisco's Golden Gate Bridge, or the Santa Fe Railway's *Super Chief.* Without the (often instinctive) design talents of these men and women, the civilized world would be mundane and, well, uncivilized.

The look and feel of a building, household appliance, or vehicle can often be as important as its functionality. There was a time when passenger trains criss-crossed America in vast numbers (an almost incomprehensible concept by today's standards, since most of the population is not old enough to recall an era when the passenger train was *the* principal form of transportation). And, until the 1930s, most of these trains were reasonably comfortable (at least those with air-conditioning, which was just catching on), functional (they reliably got you to where you were going and usually on time), and . . . depressingly mundane. Passenger cars were not much more than dark-painted steel boxes with square windows and interior appointments that could best be described as "Grandparents' Living Room Bland."

The Art Deco movement, which had its roots in the 1920s, and the subsequent coming of age for industrial designers changed all that. And—thankfully—things haven't been the same since. The application of design to form and function affected railroading, just as it would the automobile, airline, manufacturing, and construction industries. In the railroad industry, nowhere was design application more visible than in the streamliner and all of its trappings. The streamliners that began proliferating in the 1930s reflected a fascinating array of art and design, some of it understated, some of it spectacular, and almost all of it attention-getting. And, as is the case with "hang it on your wall art," there was good and not-so-good art.

Streamliner design stabilized after World War II as cost considerations and practicality began to override—or at least influence—the design factor. And then, as the 1950s progressed, nearly the whole bottom fell out of the rail passenger industry as the full impact of the burgeoning popularity of the automobile and airliner settled upon railroad management.

But as is often the case, history has come full circle. People in the transportation industry are finally beginning to realize that every form of transport has its virtues. When Amtrak assumed operation of most intercity passenger trains in 1971, the passenger train had reached its nadir. Since then, there has been a turnaround, though at times it's been a bumpy ride, and ridership—and the number of trains—overall has increased. Indeed, as the twentieth century wound down, the crescendo of people calling for improved and additional passenger services reached a new crescendo. In response, new streamliners have come on line and more are in the works. The streamlined passenger train is in vogue again!

A word about "art" as used in this book. The art of the streamliner is more than just the look of a train. Art permeated every aspect of rail passenger service, from locomotive design to the sometimes campy train ads that would appear in the *Saturday Evening Post* in the 1950s. So, in *The Art of the Streamliner,* we're going to look at more than just a train's design. We'll take you into the minds of train designers; we'll talk about colors, materials, and structural components; we'll show you dining-car china, baggage tags, and lots of train brochures and folders filled with period artistry. And we'll see how all of this tied together through the ages.

We guarantee that you will look at passenger trains with an entirely different eye.

Mike Schafer, Editor & Art Director
Andover Junction Publications
Lee, Illinois

Streamlining at its finest. The first streamlined edition of Santa Fe Railway's world-famous *Super Chief* combined state-of-the-art locomotive and railcar design, stunning exterior graphics, and captivating Native American Indian interior appointments. The train is shown posing on the outskirts of Chicago in 1937. THE HAGLEY MUSEUM AND LIBRARY

THE GENESIS TRAINS

1

TWO PIONEERS LEAD AMERICAN RAILROADS INTO STREAMLINING

In the beginning, passenger trains were entirely functional conveyances. In the late 1820s, when passengers first were commercially carried by rail, the amazing speed at which people could get from one place to another overrode the fact that the passenger carriages were unheated, had no windows or bathrooms, and rode like bucking broncos. During the ensuing 100 years or so, passengers began demanding more than speed. They wanted basic comforts and an environment that was conducive to making a long trip more like a vacation than an endurance test. Railroads complied by providing dining, lounge, and sleeping-car services—albeit with stoic, often conservative interior designs. Meanwhile, train exteriors remained functional—and therefore mundane. Not until industrial designers in the 1930s began looking at trains as art forms did a new era of rail passenger service emerge. And, it began with two little trains, each of which reflected widely disparate approaches to streamlining. Regardless, together both spurred a design movement that continues to this day.

Union Pacific's M-10000 streamliner (left) and Burlington's *Zephyr* 9900—both built in 1934—stand at Kansas City Union Station. UNION PACIFIC MUSEUM

With the advent of the 1930s, art made the leap from stationary object to moving vehicle. Nowhere was that change more evident than in American railroading, where the economic impacts of the automobile and the Great Depression had demanded a fresh start to attract passengers back to the rails. It happened with the railroad streamliner, an aerodynamically shaped, artistic statement of a train whose ultra-modern design and flashy good looks were intended to attract attention—and passengers.

What made the streamliner an art form and distinguished it from its predecessors was the influence of a new breed—the industrial designer. Never before had shape, color, texture, and theme been so integral to the completion of a train. Prior to the ascendancy of industrial design in railroading, shape had been an afterthought, dictated primarily by engineering and clearances. Color, at least for the previous 50 years, had been with few exceptions, dark: black for locomotives, dark green for passenger cars in an effort to hide the grime of railroading. Interiors featured the conservative materials of the day. Pity the passenger allergic to mohair or bored by the dark green curtains of a Pullman car.

The arrival of the industrial designer changed all this. Although designers usually were not given free reign to alter basic structures (due to manufacturing costs and engineering concerns), they accomplished amazing feats within the parameters set for them. The most dramatic changes in shape occurred on the head end as chunky steam locomotives and boxy electrics were transformed, with the help of sheet metal and welding, into bullet-shaped objects of speed and beauty. New diesels built to pull the streamliners emerged with the same attractive lines. Teardrop shapes enclosed the rear of new trains, replacing the dusty, open-platform observation car.

The use of a rainbow of new colors and metals (both exterior and interior) also set the streamliner apart from its predecessors. Interiors ran the gamut from Henry Dreyfuss' cork walls and leather seating of the *20th Century Limited* to Sterling McDonald's riot of Navajo blanketry patterns on Santa Fe's *Super Chief*. Perhaps most importantly, the shapes, colors, and finishes the designers crafted made sense—they were now a unified design, a rolling statement. The smooth shapes and bullet nose said speed; the color scheme and interiors expressed what the railroad wanted to say about itself—elegance for the New York Central, pride in its Southwest heritage for Santa Fe.

All this creativity didn't come at the expense of a deadline. The designers always worked under the gun. Renowned architect John Harbeson once estimated that he had designed over thirty trains for the Budd Company—and never had more than three weeks to create any of them. Time was money.

Before pen was put to paper, designers often rode the route the streamliner would traverse. They were educated on the history of the railroad and the places and people it served. They worked closely with the railroad's advertising department, both to ensure that the train's design matched the image the company desired and to give the railroad something to advertise.

Using an experienced staff, design firms sometimes worked around the clock to meet the deadline. Starting with geometrics to determine basic shape, they went immediately to perspectives using tracing paper and

Traditionally, the entire design of railcars had been a function of the manufacturer—which usually performed the task in a perfunctory manner with little regard for esthetics. But in the streamliner era, industrial designers were often called upon to develop inspiring car and locomotive designs. In the late 1940s, designer Brooks Stevens (center) and two associates finalize design specifications for Milwaukee Road's spectacular new Chicago–Tacoma, Washington, streamliner, the *Olympian Hiawatha*. JIM BECKWITH COLLECTION

pastels to study the effects of various color schemes on the design. Once the best ideas emerged, they were turned into a presentation that was accompanied by artist renderings, color, and material samples. Three-dimensional studies of particular features within the vehicles such as bar fronts, glass partitions, and even entire cars were created.

Based on options detailed in the presentation, the railroad and manufacturer chose a final design. Contract artists, given the general theme expected, were unleashed to create interior art. The designer then shepherded his or her concept as it evolved into an actual train. Using their experience to specify or substitute materials, designers worked hard to ensure that the final product

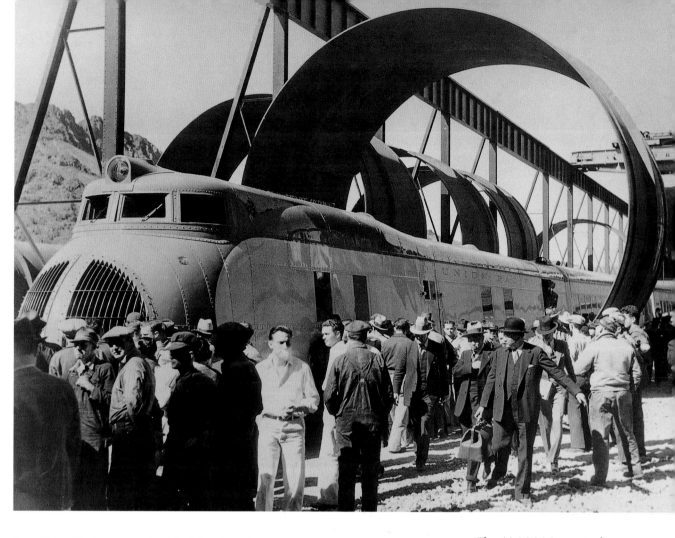

looked as good as the original drawings. John Harbeson once went to considerable lengths to find a way to panel the tight curving confines of the 1937 *Super Chief* in rare woods. Specifying a new product, a 1/85-inch wood layer on a canvas backing, he created stunning interiors and perhaps the most beautiful passenger train of all time. Brooks Stevens used his genius to craft an amazing glass-enclosed solarium for the rear of the Milwaukee Road's *Hiawatha*s. Other designers worked similar miracles using new forms of lighting and other new materials to achieve interiors and exteriors that were as innovative as they were attractive.

The brief era of the early streamliner represented a rare confluence of opportunity and talent. Through vision and hard work, the industrial designers transformed forever the image of the American passenger train, creating an icon recognized today as art.

THE FIRST STREAMLINER—UNION PACIFIC'S M-10000

The Union Pacific Railroad ushered in the era of the streamliner in February 1934 when it took delivery of a train initially known only by an alpha-numeric designation: M-10000 ("M" for "motor-powered"). Combining futuristic design worthy of a Buck Rogers movie, light weight, and high speed, the 204-foot, three-unit speedster galvanized public attention.

Built by Pullman Car & Manufacturing Company in Chicago, the stunning new train included a 600-hp distillate engine–driven power car that also contained a railway post office (RPO) and baggage area under its roof. Passengers were accommodated in a 60-seat coach and a 56-seat coach-buffet. Meals, dispensed from a tea cart dispatched from the buffet by an attendant, were consumed at one's seat.

The M-10000 created a sensation everywhere it went during its multi-month tour of the U.S. in 1934. Crowds swarm the train during a special stopover at Hoover Dam in Nevada, where the M-10000 posed within a section of the monstrous water-flow pipes used in the dam's construction.
UNION PACIFIC MUSEUM

PROGRESS

UNION PACIFIC
THE OVERLAND ROUTE

"THE LAUREL WREATH FOR TRANSPORTATION PROGRESS MUST GO TO THE UNION PACIFIC RAILROAD"
—George Creel in Collier's, August 5, 1933

UNION PACIFIC

LEFT: The cover of the "Progress" folder published by Union Pacific for the 1933–34 Century of Progress Exhibition in Chicago featured the distinctive countenance of the railroad's new M-10000 streamliner against line drawings that depicted the evolution of travel across the American West. MIKE SCHAFER COLLECTION

BELOW: Unfolded, the "Progress" promotional piece revealed a side elevation and floor plan of the M-10000. As originally designed and built, the train had four cars, but the sleeping car was removed prior to the train's 1934 tour. MIKE SCHAFER COLLECTION

FACING PAGE: Wedged in the rounded tail end of the M-10000 was a compact buffet-kitchen from which passengers could buy refreshments to take back to their seats. Coach seats featured fold-down trays. UNION PACIFIC MUSEUM COLLECTION, IMAGE NO. 87657-C

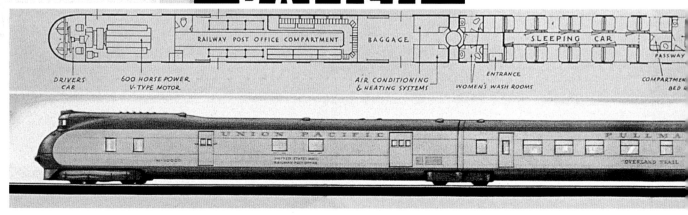

DRIVERS CAB — 600 HORSE POWER V-TYPE MOTOR — RAILWAY POST OFFICE COMPARTMENT — BAGGAGE — AIR CONDITIONING & HEATING SYSTEMS — WOMEN'S WASH ROOMS — ENTRANCE — SLEEPING CAR — PASSWAY — COMPARTMENT BED — UNION PACIFIC — PULLMAN — OVERLAND TRAIL

The tiny train's rounded contours (as a result of tests of a model of the train in a wind tunnel) immediately differentiated it from the standard railcars of the day. Constructed of aluminum, a lightweight, strong metal, the entire train weighed in at just 124 tons, including its power plant—less than a third of the weight of some of the larger steam locomotives of its day. Although the M-10000's spartan interior was relatively unremarkable, its bright Armour yellow and leaf brown exterior (yellow, for safety) drew immediate attention.

Smooth shapes, lightweight metals, and bright colors would all become regular design features of future streamliners. But this first streamliner also included some elements that would vanish as new designs emerged with time. The gas-powered engine would quickly be overshadowed by more reliable diesels. The train's height of approximately eleven feet was lower than normal by up to two feet. Its "fish-belly" shape—wider at the bottom, tapering in at the top—made it difficult to maximize the utility of interior space. Finally, the train was articulated. The three cars of the M-10000 were semi-permanently coupled over a shared set of wheels (called trucks). While a normal three-car train would have had six

trucks (two per car), the new streamliner had a total of four—at a considerable savings in weight. But articulation also made the train inflexible to ridership fluctuations and made the addition of extra cars a major undertaking. Although many early streamliners shared some of these same characteristics, they would disappear with time as better designs emerged.

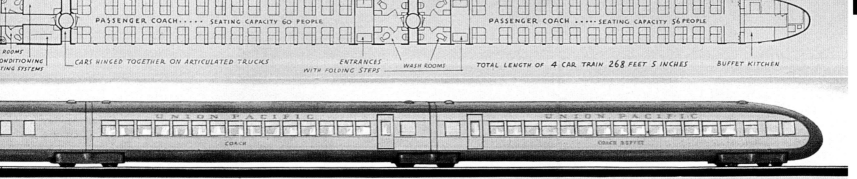

RIGHT: As with UP's M-10000 streamliner, *Zephyr* 9900 yielded much promotional material. This folder, done with black, red, and silver ink, was assembled for the 1934 Century of Progress Exposition in Chicago, where *Zephyr* 9900 would end its famed dawn-to-dusk Denver–Chicago speed run (1,015.4 miles in 13 hours, five minutes) in May of that year. MIKE SCHAFER COLLECTION

Wings to the Iron Horse

Burlington

THE WEST WIND

Zephyr

Burlington Pioneers Again ═══➤ First Diesel Streamline Train

The interior of the 9900's coach, shown following the train's complete restoration in 1997, reveals the simple, modern look and light colors that would replace the more ornate styles of the 1920s. Northern Rail Car of Milwaukee handled the three-year revamping while the Grainger Corporation of Skokie, Illinois, sponsored the restoration project for the train's owner, Chicago's famed Museum of Science and Industry. MIKE SCHAFER

The social center of Chicago, Burlington & Quincy's new *Zephyr* was the train's lounge observation car. Unlike Union Pacific's M-10000 streamliner, whose windowless rounded tail end housed a kitchen buffet, the 9900 used the area for scenery viewing. Chrome and polished aluminum trim and chair frames added more of an Art Deco touch to this area of the train than to the coach and coach-buffet sections. MIKE SCHAFER

Perhaps the M-10000's most important contribution was in attracting public attention to the streamliner. Traveling on a nationwide tour from Atlantic to Pacific, "Little Zip," as UP crews called the train, was exhibited in 68 cities and visited by more than 1.1 million people, including Franklin D. Roosevelt whose administration was particularly interested in spurring exactly the kind of progress and private enterprise the new train represented. Eventually the little pioneer entered regular service as *The Streamliner* between Kansas City, Topeka, and Salina, Kansas, at a regularly scheduled average speed of about a mile a minute, including stops. (The M-10000 was easily capable of speeds in excess of 100 MPH.)

BURLINGTON'S ZEPHYR 9900— THE FIRST DIESEL STREAMLINER

Like its M-10000 counterpart, the Burlington *Zephyr* had an instant impact on all who encountered it during the simpler times of the 1930s. Picture yourself trackside at some rural location in eastern Colorado on the morning of May 26, 1934, the day of the *Zephyr*'s landmark nonstop run. Suddenly, off to the west, a boiling cloud of dust appears, surrounding a bouncing headlight beam. Within seconds a shining, silver streak like nothing you have ever seen rockets past at 109 MPH. The lack of a steam engine on the head end, its low-slung form, slanted nose, and shimmering silver skin are totally foreign. In seconds it's gone from sight. But, you have just witnessed history in the making.

The train will gather an increasing amount of attention as it speeds east. In rural Iowa and Illinois, fire sirens scream and church bells peal to announce its approach. Thousands, including President Roosevelt, sit glued to their radios listening to its progress. That evening the *Zephyr* will roll to a stop in Chicago, having covered the 1,015 miles between Denver and the Windy City in an amazing 13 hours and five minutes, setting a series of new world speed records.

The headline-grabbing *Zephyr* arrived on the scene in April 1934, a month and a half after the M-10000. Unlike the Union Pacific train, it embodied two important features that remain key elements of passenger-train design

Zephyr 9900—known as the *Pioneer Zephyr* when this photo was taken on its last day of service in March 1960—stands at Burlington's Omaha station. The nose of *Zephyr* 9900 and several of its progeny had a simple sloping shape to reduce air resistance. Unfortunately, the design also made engine crews especially vulnerable in collisions with wayward motor vehicles at grade crossings or with other trains (and the 9900 did indeed suffer from several collisions during its 26-year career, including a deadly head-on with a freight train in 1939 that ripped the whole crew cab off the train). Later designs moved locomotive cabs high above a bulbous nose. JIM NEUBAUER

PAUL PHILIPPE CRET

Born in Lyons, France, in 1876, Paul Cret immigrated to the United States in the early 1900s. Known as one of the foremost practitioners of the Beaux-Arts style, Cret abandoned this traditional approach for modernism by the late 1920s. As a key figure in the evolution of modern design, his metamorphosis made him one of the most important figures in American architecture. Among Cret's notable contributions were the Folger Shakespeare Library on Capitol Hill in Washington, D.C., and much of the campus of the University of Texas at Austin.

Cret also played a large role in creating perhaps the greatest modern American railroad depot—Cincinnati Union Terminal. Hired by the terminal company to modernize and improve on the conservative design concept of the architectural firm of Fellheimer & Wagner, Cret gave the structure a timeless Art Deco look that mesmerizes visitors to the building—now a museum and Amtrak station—to this day.

Head of the School of Architecture at the University of Pennsylvania, Cret was associated with the Philadelphia firm of Harbeson, Hough, Livingston & Larson. In the mid-1930s, Cret and his associates provided architectural support to the fledgling Budd Company (also of Philadelphia) which was involved in the development of a new concept—the railroad streamliner. Searching for a way to strengthen the thin stainless-steel sides that were going to be applied to Chicago, Burlington & Quincy's first streamliner in 1934, Cret gave Budd's trains their graceful fluted exteriors—a design that was later copied by other builders.

His firm's work on Burlington's *Denver Zephyr* of 1936 and Santa Fe's 1937 *Super Chief* produced two of the most beautiful streamliners ever created. Both trains' interiors could literally be described as works of art. Paul Cret died in September 1945.

Paul Cret helped develop a fluting process for stainless steel that not only strengthened fabricated railcar sides, but established a timeless, modern look to passenger cars. MIKE SCHAFER

today—diesel power for locomotion and stainless steel for construction. The sleek *Zephyr* was designed by an aeronautical engineer, Albert Dean (working for the train's builder, the Edward G. Budd Manufacturing Company), and decorated by architects John Harbeson and Paul Cret. Its aerodynamically sloped nose inspired the classic shapes of later diesel locomotives, and its gracefully fluted sides (so shaped for strength as well as beauty) encouraged a legion of similar passenger train equipment.

Designed as a three-car, articulated train, the 197-foot-long streamliner originally included a Railway Post Office (RPO), a baggage coach, and a coach-parlor observation car. Like the M-10000, the *Zephyr*'s cars were smaller than a standard railroad car, contained modest interior appointments, and was punctuated by a tear-drop shape. Unlike the Union Pacific train, the *Zephyr*'s rear car featured a solarium where passengers could watch the scenery rocketing past their window. The streamlined observation car was born.

After a national tour and a role in the Hollywood movie *Silver Streak*, Burlington's new train became the first regularly scheduled diesel-powered, stainless-steel streamliner on November 11, 1934, entering service on a Lincoln–Omaha–Kansas City route. As new *Zephyr*s came on line, *Zephyr 9900* was aptly renamed *Pioneer Zephyr* to differentiate it from new sister trains.

EPILOGUE

The two popular pioneers met very different ends. The Union Pacific M-10000 was withdrawn from service in December 1941. A victim of its own radical design, the train was scrapped in 1942 as a valuable wartime source of aluminum. The amazing *Zephyr* 9900 remained in regular service (stainless steel not being as recyclable as aluminum) until March 20, 1960, when it was retired and donated to Chicago's Museum of Science and Industry. Following a three-year restoration completed in 1997, it can be seen there today, symbol of an entire generation in which Art Deco design and radical engineering blended seamlessly to create rolling art. Each train inspired the creation of hundreds of other streamliners operating from Atlantic to Pacific and from Mexico to Canada.

Still looking shiny and modern after 26 years and millions of miles of service, the *Pioneer Zephyr* (a.k.a. *Zephyr 9900*), heads across the Mississippi River at Burlington, Iowa, on March 20, 1960. The train is en route from Omaha to Chicago as a special run for press and railroad historians and fans—it is the 9900's last revenue run. Shortly after, the train was presented to Chicago's Museum of Science and Industry, where today it enjoys a prominent, newly developed display location. JIM NEUBAUER

FLEDGLING STREAMLINERS

② **TRAINS THAT EXPANDED THE STREAMLINER MOVEMENT**

The early success and amazing amount of public interest generated by *Zephyr* 9900 and the M-10000 led the Burlington and Union Pacific to dramatically expand the streamliner concept and encouraged other railroads to conceive their own new trains of wide-ranging designs. While some were near-carbon copies of the diesel-powered *Zephyr*, other offerings were multiple-car lightweight trains hauled by attractively streamlined steam locomotives. At least one was designed and built by a former manufacturer of airships! As a whole, the group of streamliners that emerged after the *Zephyr* and M-10000 were custom-designed. However, as new streamliners began to cover longer distances, full dining rooms, sleeping accommodations, and sparkling lounge facilities were added. Mechanical and design features literally evolved from one train set to the next as locomotive and passenger car builders learned from each successive experience. The fascinating concept of streamlining was in full bloom and proceeding boldly ahead into uncharted territory.

SPEED COMFORT BEAUTY POWER ACHIEVEMENT

BURLINGTON

ZEPHYRUS

Burlington Route

Burlington Route

TAGE FROM THE GODS

Cover of booklet released by the Chicago, Burlington & Quincy to publicize its new *Twin Zephyr* streamliners of 1936. MIKE SCHAFER COLLECTION

WAY OF THE ZEPHYRS

Several months after its breathtaking dawn-to-dusk sprint between Denver and the Century of Progress Exposition at Chicago on May 26, 1934, shovel-nosed *Zephyr* 9900 completed a test run on the Burlington's 437-mile route between Chicago and Minneapolis/ St. Paul—the Twin Cities—that was five hours faster than the fastest steam-powered train on the line. The stainless-steel die was cast: the railroad immediately ordered two additional three-unit trains from the Budd Company and Electro-Motive based on the original *Zephyr* design, and the first streamliner brand was born.

The new twin trains were aptly christened as the *Twin Zephyrs*. Launched with a publicity run for movie newsreel cameras the following April, in which 44 pairs of identical twins split up and rode the two trains into Chicago, the once-a-day each-way *Twin Zephyrs* became so popular that another daily round-trip for each was added less than two months after their introduction. New, longer trains were ordered for the route.

The two new seven-car trainsets taking over the Chicago–Twin Cities run in December 1936 began to bridge the gap between novelty and luxury. The new trains continued the Greek mythology theming that focused on Zephyrus, God of the West Wind. However, instead of just two passenger cars compartmentalized into different interior areas as the 9900 and original *Twin Zephyrs* had been configured, the new trains— labeled "Trains of the Gods and Goddesses" (one train featured the names of Greek gods; the other, Greek goddesses)—offered separate "feature" cars like a dining car, mid-train cocktail bar, and end-of-train parlor-lounges. With names like *Ceres, Venus, Apollo,* and (on a power car, naturally) *Pegasus* emblazoned on their sides, the cars

Most early streamliners were built as trainsets comprised of permanently coupled cars, usually "articulated" in nature. This closeup of two adjoining cars of an early Burlington *Zephyr* illustrates articulation, in which adjacent cars share a common wheel assembly ("truck"). This arrangement reduced the train's overall weight and provided a smoother ride. However, the main drawback of this system is lack of flexibility in accommodating passengers, as extra cars could not be added to meet peak demands. Also, if one car required special repairs, then the whole trainset had to be removed from service (and usually substituted with a steam-powered conventional train). For these two reasons, articulated train design fell into disfavor by the end of the 1930s on most railroads. ALVIN SCHULTZE

THE ART OF THE STREAMLINER

Dining on *The New Twin Zephyrs* is a festive occasion representing a delightful combination of harmonious surroundings, attentive service and highly skilled cookery.

LEFT: A "cosmopolitan rendezvous" is how Burlington copywriters described the 1936 *Twin Zephyr* lounge cars. This page from the beautiful *Heritage From the Gods* brochure shows a bright, modern lounge whose only detraction seems to be the school-bus-style seating in the table area. MIKE SCHAFER COLLECTION

BELOW: After a decade of service on the Chicago Twin Cities route, the 1936-edition *Twin Zephyrs* were reassigned to the Chicago–Omaha–Lincoln route as the *Nebraska Zephyrs*, one of which is shown at Albia, Iowa, in 1967, shortly before it was retired. BOB JOHNSTON

JOHN FREDERICK HARBESON

Born in 1888, John Harbeson served as the principal of a Philadelphia firm run by Paul Cret (page 16) that provided architectural design for a vast majority of the streamliners produced by the Edward G. Budd Manufacturing Company (later known simply as the Budd Company) between 1934 and the 1950s. Harbeson's first effort involving streamliners was the interior design of the landmark *Zephyr* 9900 of 1934. He is perhaps best known for the design of Chicago, Burlington & Quincy's magnificent *Denver Zephyr* of 1936—a train he readily acknowledged as his favorite project. Along with Sterling McDonald, Harbeson was also responsible for designing the interiors of Santa Fe's stunning *Super Chief* of 1937 (chapter 5). During the post-World War II era, he was credited with the design of one of the greatest streamliners ever conceived, the *California Zephyr*. John Harbeson died in 1986.

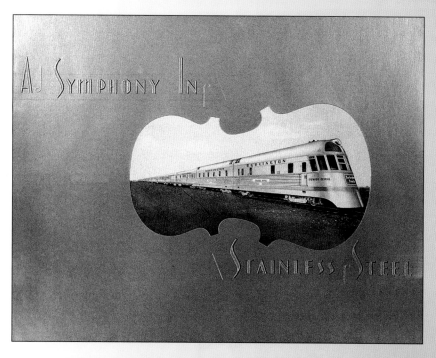

The brochure released to market the new (in 1936) *Denver Zephyrs*—which were styled by John Harbeson—was simple yet very elegant. The cover was silver embossed with "A Symphony In Stainless Steel," and a black-and-white photo of one of the new speedsters was framed in a violin-shaped opening. Like the train it touted, the brochure was a work of art. Harbeson felt that the *Denver Zephyr* was his favorite styling assignment. JOE WELSH COLLECTION

incorporated onboard amenities and the freedom to roam that travelers had come to expect on the best conventional steam-powered trains of the day.

Also in 1936, Burlington's pair of 12-car overnight *Denver Zephyrs* upped the luxury quotient by offering four sleeping cars with a total of six different kinds of accommodations, including economy "chambrettes" for single travelers and drawing rooms for three. Powered by a two-unit shovel-nosed diesel power-car set, the inside of each *Denver Zephyr* was light and airy, with touches of rich mahogany in the lounge, hall, and dining areas. Reading lights next to the windows in the sleepers had an alternate blue night-light setting, and outlets for 110-volt electric razors in coach and sleeping-car dressing rooms signified use of the latest technology.

The *Zephyr* artistry of Paul Cret and John Harbeson set a new standard of train design in the mid 1930s that looked just as fresh and exciting some 30 years later when the 1936 *Twin Zephyrs* and *Denver Zephyrs* finished their Burlington careers in *Nebraska Zephyr* and *Texas Zephyr* service, respectively. (In 1947 the *Twin Zephyr* trainsets—displaced by new *Twin Zephyr* equipment—had been moved to Chicago–Omaha–Lincoln service and renamed. In 1956, the original *Denver Zephyr* equipment, likewise displaced by new equipment, had been reassigned as the Denver–Dallas *Texas Zephyr*.)

Zephyr 9900 and the first (1935) *Twin Zephyrs* were joined by other, short trains that proudly rolled into the 1950s in various routes and services marketed as the *Mark Twain, Sam Houston, Silver Streak, Ozark State,* and *General Pershing Zephyrs*. Today, the goddess *Twin Zephyr* trainset (minus its power car, however) from 1936 can be seen at the Illinois Railway Museum and on occasional special outings; the gods set was still in regular service as of 2000, speeding passengers between various Saudi Arabian destinations. The most historic of all the early *Zephyr* streamliners, No. 9900 (later also known as the *Pioneer Zephyr*), serves as one of the grand displays of Chicago's Museum of Science and Industry. There, patrons may view firsthand the designwork of Albert Dean, Paul Cret, and John Harbeson, for the train has been restored to as-delivered condition inside and out.

THE "CITY" STREAMLINERS

At the same time *Zephyr* 9900 debuted, the Union Pacific was so confident that its new M-10000 streamliner would be a success that it ordered a second streamlined trainset from Pullman-Standard and Electro-Motive before the M-10000 had even been delivered. After a record-setting Chicago-to-Los Angeles run, the new seven-car speedster—designated as the M-10001—was re-engined and entered regular service on May 5, 1935, as the *City of Portland*, "sailing" from Chicago and Portland six times each month in each direction.

Retaining the low profile, sloping sides, and the nose-to-tail features of the M-10000 as well as the original's leaf brown and Armour yellow exterior, the air-conditioned *City of Portland* was the first streamliner to incorporate both a full dining-lounge car, three sleeping cars (with

UNION PACIFIC STREAMLINER "CITY OF PORTLAND"

ABOVE: Union Pacific's M-10001 streamliner was christened in 1935 as the *City of Portland*. The overall design closely followed that of UP's original streamliner, the M-10000. JOE WELSH COLLECTION

LEFT: Sloped car sides are a clue that this is the interior of one of Union Pacific's early M-series streamliners—in this case the diner-lounge for the 1935 edition of the *City of Portland*. Stainless-steel trim was *de riguer* on early streamliners, and etched-glass partitions reduced the "tunnel effect" inherent in passenger railcars. Chair upholstery featured an Art Deco pattern. UNION PACIFIC MUSEUM COLLECTION, IMAGE NO. 14-271

NORTH WESTERN — UNION PACIFIC'S
FAMOUS FLEET OF
Streamliners

"CITY OF DENVER"
DAILY SERVICE · NO EXTRA FARE

"CITY OF LOS ANGELES"
FIVE ROUND TRIPS A MONTH · EXTRA FARE

"CITY OF SAN FRANCISCO"
FIVE ROUND TRIPS A MONTH · EXTRA FARE

"CITY OF PORTLAND"
FIVE ROUND TRIPS A MONTH · NO EXTRA FARE

"CITY OF SALINA"
DAILY SERVICE · NO EXTRA FARE

COMPLETE INFORMATION & SCHEDULES INSIDE

ABOVE: Brochures issued in 1937 for Union Pacific's growing fleet of streamliners—operated jointly with the Chicago & North Western Railway between Chicago and Omaha—played on the trains' yellow-and-brown livery. MIKE SCHAFER COLLECTION

BELOW: One of the most remarkable feature cars of any of the early streamliners was the lounge-observation car known as *Copper King*, assigned to the *City of Los Angeles* in 1938. The unusual car featured porthole Polaroid windows. Using handcranks on each window, passengers could rotate the special polarized-glass windows to reduce glare from outside light sources. The round windows gave the car a space-age look, albeit at the expense of window-viewing area. UNION PACIFIC MUSEUM COLLECTION, IMAGE NO. **60-480**

sections, compartments, and bedrooms), as well as a buffet-coach and Railway Post Office/baggage car.

The interior color scheme was predominantly in shades of blue with a vaulted ceiling of off-white that progressed down the car sides, with aluminum trim, to light blue and then dark blue below the windows. The radio-equipped lounge was separated from the dining portion of the car by etched-glass panels. Coach seats reclined and Pullman section sleeping accommodations featured not only the traditional green modesty curtains but sliding aluminum doors for additional privacy.

On the heels of the *City of Portland*, Union Pacific introduced the *City of Los Angeles* on May 15, 1936. The new train duplicated the *City of Portland* except that it contained an additional locomotive and (eventually) 10 other cars articulated in pairs instead of all permanently linked together. Several months later, an 11-car *City of*

GOLDEN
LIMITED BRAND
PEARS

PACKED & SHIPPED BY
MYRON ROOT & CO. INC.
MEDFORD, OREGON

CONTENTS ½ BUSHEL

San Francisco debuted on a five-times-per-month sailing schedule in each direction, with interior decor similar to its two Chicago–West Coast predecessors.

But the designs were gradually changing. Cars of both the *City of Los Angeles* and *City of San Francisco* were wider and higher than those on the *City of Portland*, although they still retained the inwardly sloping sides of the earliest train. The *City of San Francisco*'s diesel locomotive front had been radically redesigned and now resembled an automobile nose with a long hood and a large grille, a design repeated on the locomotives powering the two new 10-car trainsets also being launched as

the *City of Denver*, operating overnight every night between Chicago and Denver. Yet, the *City of Denver*'s cars were wider and taller, with straight sides adding more interior room.

Perhaps the Denver train's most unusual innovation was the "Frontier Shack" lounge designed by Walt Kuhn, where walls and floors of unfinished wood planking, roof beams made out of logs, hanging electric lights passing as kerosene lamps, and mounted animal heads and rifles all evoked a rustic Western atmosphere—the perfect place to down a sarsaparilla heading for the untamed wilds of Colorado. The *City of Denver*'s attractive diner-lounge

Early streamliners were very much in the public eye, and some companies used their imagery to promote products. To promote its "Golden Limited" brand pears, the fruit crates of produce distributor Myron Root featured this label bearing a likeness of an early Union Pacific streamliner. MIKE SCHAFER COLLECTION

COLORADO

This brochure cover for the original *City of Denver* featured stylistic artwork that was almost timeless. The artwork would look as good a quarter century or more later as it did when first issued in the late 1930s. As is the nature of promotional products, however, exaggeration for the sake of impact and sales was simply an accepted practice. The scene implies that the *City of Denver* wheeled amongst the majestic peaks of the Colorado Rockies. In reality, however, the train (as well as its ilk—Burlington's *Denver Zephyr,* Rock Island's *Rocky Mountain Rocket,* and Missouri Pacific's *Colorado Eagle*) never got any closer than a dozen miles or so from the Rockies. As seasoned travelers know, Denver lies at the foot of—not in—America's best-known mountain range. JOE WELSH COLLECTION

AND THE *Streamliner* CITY OF DENVER

UNION PACIFIC

THE OVERLAND ROUTE

contained wood-grain walls, aluminum trim, etched glass, and a bar front covered in redwood burl. Pullmans and coaches featured pleasing pastel color schemes. For the first time, upper berths in the sleeping cars had their own little windows. Finally, the *City of Denver*'s sleeper-lounge observation car was punctuated by a glass-enclosed solarium at its very end—a welcome departure from all previous UP streamliners, whose windowless rear ends had housed a buffet-kitchen.

Taking tail-car design to the next level was the *Copper King*, introduced in 1938 on the second edition of the *City of Los Angeles*. Rebuilt from a lowly baggage-mail car from the 1936 *City of San Francisco*, the *Copper King*'s interior walls were of satin-finished copper sheathing while copper and green hues were used for the carpet and drapes. Twenty-nine large, round Polaroid windows could be adjusted by patrons to filter light and glare.

ABOVE: While nearly every streamliner of the Depression era played on the futuristic theme in some way, the "Frontier Shack" lounges of the 1936 *City of Denver* were quite retro, with their rustic Western motif of a bygone era. UNION PACIFIC MUSEUM COLLECTION, IMAGE NO. 6-10-1936

LEFT: The power car of the 1936 *City of Denver* featured automobile styling, no doubt the influence of builder Electro-Motive, a subsidiary of General Motors. The train is shown east of Denver (note the Rocky Mountains in the distance) in 1942. UNION PACIFIC MUSEUM COLLECTION, IMAGE NO. 02

SPEED

Designed for speed—and rapid acceleration—The Comet was planned to one of the *safest* trains in existen Constructed of Duralumin, one of strongest and lightest of metals, with center of gravity nearly 25 inches lo than ordinary trains, it *hugs the r* develops little sway and makes cu imperceptible . . . yet it weighs than half of a conventional type with equal seating capacity.

OF YANKEES AND COMETS IN NEW ENGLAND

Not content to allow their Western and Midwestern cousins all the glory, three New England railroads inaugurated two completely different lightweight streamliners in 1935. In February, allies Boston & Maine and Maine Central took delivery of a virtual twin to *Zephyr* 9900 (with carbodies by Budd and power plant by Electro-Motive) and dubbed it the *Flying Yankee*. The three-car, stainless-steel, diesel-powered streamliner entered service between Boston, Massachusetts, and Bangor, Maine, and was an immediate success. Featuring a combination power car/baggage-buffet, a coach, and a coach-observation car, the train's interiors were finished in pastel hues. Passengers were served meals on trays at their seats.

Ironically, the *Yankee*'s small capacity and articulated design lacked the flexibility to handle heavy wartime passenger demand, and it was bumped to runs less prone to widely fluctuating patronage and operated under the names *Cheshire* or *Minute Man*. Retired in 1957, the train remains on display today near Crawford Notch, New Hampshire.

If the *Flying Yankee* traced its pedigree to a builder that would dominate the streamlined era, the New York, New Haven & Hartford's first entry into complete streamlined trains was the product of a firm that would build only one train. The *Comet* was created by the Goodyear-Zeppelin Corporation, an American/German consortium attempting to break into railcar manufacturing in the wake of the demise of the airship market in the 1930s. Sporting porpoise-nosed power cars with robot-like faces sandwiching a non-powered coach, the bi-directional workhorse rode on a total of four trucks, its rounded car bodies clearing the rails by a mere 10 inches. The total weight of the three-car aluminum-alloy train was an amazingly light 126 tons. By contrast, one traditional heavyweight dining car might weigh up to 90 tons. Debuting on New Haven's relatively short Providence–Boston run (43 miles) in June 1935 without any of the onboard amenities offered on other lightweights of the era, the 160-seat blue-and-aluminum streamliner, with its wide picture windows, air conditioning, and indirect lighting, was a welcome departure for New Englanders used to soot and cinders.

Like the *Flying Yankee*, the articulated three-car *Comet* was unable to be easily expanded to meet peak demand, a drawback that would eventually doomed fixed articulated trainsets nationwide (though, interestingly, this format would return in the 1950s and again in the 1990s). Demoted to local service in 1943, the *Comet* was retired in September 1951. As an amalgamation, Goodyear-Zeppelin had disappeared in 1941.

FACING PAGE CENTER AND BELOW: The New York, New Haven & Hartford Railroad spared little expense in producing this elaborate folder for its Goodyear-Zeppelin *Comet*, another new streamliner to hit New England rails in 1935. As with the *Flying Yankee* and various Burlington *Zephyr* folders, silver ink was employed to represent new alloy metals being used on the trains. Inside the *Comet* brochure were cutaway views of the power car and coaches. MIKE SCHAFER COLLECTION

SAFETY

werful headlights flood the tracks and
ertical pencil beam on the roof points
ward, warning motorists long before
e long range sirens can be heard.

e latest type brakes, doors with fold-
steps in the center of the car, which
st be closed before the train can
ve, combine with many innovations
give The New Haven the finest and the
est streamlined train the world has seen.

THE COMET...

The new *Rebel* streamliners of the Gulf, Mobile & Northern were practical in that they were non-articulated. Cars could easily be switched into or out of the train to accommodate fluctuating passenger demand. This watercolor shows the *Rebel* at Murphysboro, Illinois, in the 1940s on the tracks of new owner Gulf, Mobile & Ohio. WATERCOLOR BY MIKE SCHAFER

REBELS IN THE SOUTH

Unlike the larger steam railroads that turned to the internal-combustion engine in earnest with the onset of the Great Depression, the Gulf, Mobile & Northern began replacing its chugging coal burners on light-density runs in the mid-1920s with gas-electric railcars. Of particular note was a boxy-looking motorcar and three trailing coaches delivered by streetcar manufacturer Brill Motorcar Company in 1930. This train, the *St. Tammany Special*, would set the stage for GM&N's streamlined era with its distinctive silver paint and red stripe through the windows of all four cars. The GM&N—having lightweight-train proponent and Burlington President Ralph Budd on its board of directors—also acquired a bullet-shaped, self-propelled single-car

"Railplane" from Pullman Car & Manufacturing before inaugurating the first streamlined train in the South, the *Rebel*, between Jackson, Tennessee, and New Orleans, in July 1935.

Built of aluminum sheathing on a Cor-Ten steel frame by American Car & Foundry and designed by up-and coming industrial stylist Otto Kuhler, the two low-slung *Rebel* sets were the first non-articulated lightweight streamliners: each car had the traditional two independent wheelsets instead of sharing one with its neighbor car. This permitted a second coach to be carried between Jackson, Mississippi, and New Orleans, the most heavily traveled portion of the run. The power car featured a diesel power plant manufactured by the American Locomotive Company.

Doorways were located in the center of each car to help divide the train into varied-use compartments and facilitate segregated seating. The rounded rear observation's brightly colored interior was staffed by a hostess—one of the first instances of train hostess service in America—and featured a ceiling that resembled the inside of a dirigible, while in front of the outside door six sections and a drawing room were provided for overnight passengers. Another *Rebel* joined the fleet in 1938, offering connecting service to Mobile, Alabama. In 1942, the trains were renovated and placed on St. Louis–New Orleans schedules after the GM&N had been merged with the Mobile & Ohio to form the Gulf, Mobile & Ohio Railroad. The innovative, lightweight trains were withdrawn from service in 1954 after successfully, and economically, serving the rural Deep South for many years.

AN ART DECO DIAMOND

Farther north, the Illinois Central had also been considering how to increase speed, reduce costs, and bring customers back to the rails in the highly competitive Chicago–St. Louis market as early as 1932. IC considered buying a virtual carbon copy of the successful M-10000 trainset that Pullman and Electro-Motive had built for the UP in 1934, but instead purchased the *Green Diamond* of 1936, which—though produced by those same manufacturers—had a noticeably different flair. From the front, it was a toothy mix of the UP train's grille and the high, squinty cab of power cars being built

by EMC at the time for later Union Pacific trains. However, unlike the *Rebel, Flying Yankee,* and *Comet,* the *Diamond* was a full-size train, with baggage-mail, full coach, dinette coach, and diner-lounge-observation cars of standard railroad-car proportions sitting well off the rail, and a power car as tall as a medium-sized steam locomotive.

Long before the streamliner era, the Illinois Central Railroad had employed a green diamond for its company herald, so the name *Green Diamond*—as well as a green-color theme—seemed logical for its new Chicago–Springfield–St. Louis streamliner. Indeed, the entire *Green Diamond* was painted in a two-tone green livery that understated the imposing proportions of the new train. This elaborate folder that accompanied the *Diamond*'s 1936 debut featured a two-foot long artist's rendering of the speedster. HERB DANNEMAN REPRODUCTION, MIKE SCHAFER COLLECTION

The *Green Diamond's* diner-lounge-observation car featured a wealth of Art Deco nicely complemented by comfy plush chairs that would have been right at home in a palatial mansion. STEVE SMEDLEY COLLECTION

But Art Deco styling–particularly inside–helped make up for a relative lack of sleekness. On the power car, dark and lighter shades of green were separated by curved white and red striping that then traveled below the windows all the way back along the train to wrap around the rear car. Similarly painted or aluminum-molded "wings" of curving, parallel lines accenting the interior walls also suggested speed, as did rounded ashtrays and elliptical lamps in the lounge, panels in the kitchen pantry, and

even wavy lines on public address loudspeakers overhead. Non-glare lighting hidden in overhead ductwork spread a warm glow at night. The style was coupled with speed: with a schedule of less than five hours, the *Green Diamond* was the fastest train between Chicago and St. Louis on any railroad until the equipment was demoted to the short-lived New Orleans–Jackson, Mississippi, *Miss Lou* in 1947. Three years later, after recurring mechanical problems, it was scrapped.

ROYAL BLUE AND ABE

Unlike many of its early counterparts that relied on fixed, articulated train sets, the Baltimore & Ohio Railroad in 1935 took delivery of two non-articulated lightweight streamliners from the same builder of the *Rebels*, American Car & Foundry. One set of equipment, built of Cor-Ten steel and christened *Abraham Lincoln*, was assigned to the Chicago–St. Louis run on B&O subsidiary Alton Railroad. The second, the aluminum-alloy *Royal Blue*, was assigned to B&O-Reading Company's Washington, D.C.—Jersey City, New Jersey, route. Full-sized like the *Green Diamond*, the trains were powered by regular locomotives, including the first self-contained passenger diesel locomotive ever built, Electro-Motive box-cab No. 50.

Similarly designed, both trains' two coaches provided extra wide seats that rotated in pairs and a diner-tavern car that contained not only formal dining tables but also a less-formal lunch counter—a popular improvement that would be repeated in countless future streamliners right up through the year 2000. The buffet-lounge car featured plush seats, and the two parlor cars offered single reclining seats as well as a private drawing room. The round-end parlor observation car contained yet another lounge at the rear of the train, where passengers in traditional easy chairs could view the passing scenery through

Shortly after its 1935 inaugural, B&O's *Royal Blue* streamliner hustles through Bayonne, New Jersey, behind new box-cab diesel No. 50. Although decidedly unstreamlined, the 50 was considered to be the first independent diesel passenger locomotive. The *Royal Blue* itself was a precursor of future streamliners, with individual cars and standard car proportions. HERBERT H. HARWOOD

ABOVE: B&O's second *Royal Blue* comprised 1920s-era standard cars that had been streamlined and modernized by Pullman and B&O's Mount Clare Shops in Baltimore. The interior of the second *Royal Blue* observation lounge shows the generous use of tubular chrome steel in the fixtures. Note "The Royal Blue" lettering on the top of the rear wall. B&O, WILLIAM F. HOWES JR. COLLECTION

BELOW: The exterior of the *Royal Blue* lounge observation car whose interior is pictured above. Rounded roofs and skirting helped hide the real age and standard-era heritage of this and other cars remodeled for *Royal Blue* service in 1937. WILLIAM HOWES JR. COLLECTION

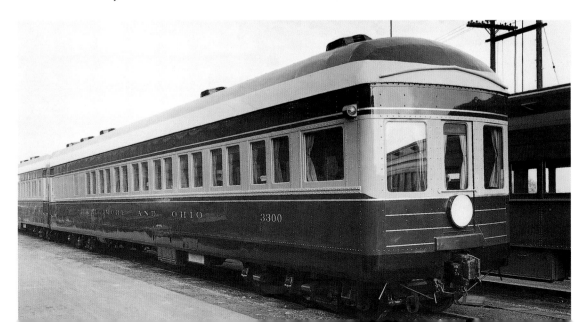

BELOW: Baltimore & Ohio's original two American Car & Foundry streamliners are represented on the cover of this rare brochure shortly after both had migrated to the Alton Railroad. MIKE SCHAFER COLLECTION

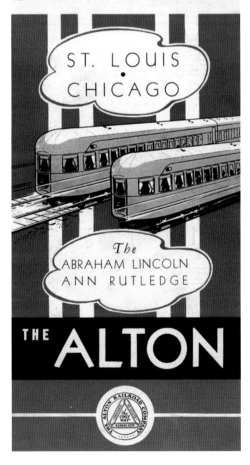

curtained windows. As would be expected, both trains were cloaked in B&O's signature color of royal blue with gold striping.

B&O quickly became disenchanted with the general ride quality of the aluminum consist, so it was sent packing to stepchild Alton while a modernized heavyweight *Royal Blue*—wearing a new blue-and-gray livery inspired by Otto Kuhler—took its place in the Northeast. Regardless, the two lightweights worked side by side for many years on the Alton and successor Gulf, Mobile & Ohio as the *Abraham Lincoln* and the *Ann Rutledge*. One of the trainsets—whose parlor observation car can be seen today at the National Museum of Transportation near St. Louis—remained in daily service into the late 1960s.

THE HOMEGROWN MERCURY

Before the advent of planes that could fly over Lake Erie, the New York Central's heavily-traveled Detroit–Cleveland route was in desperate need of some pizzazz: a fast train for businessmen at the beginning and end of each day. Rather than go for an all-new approach, which would cost time and money, the frugal NYC chose to scrounge the property and mold what it found into its "new" *Mercury* streamliner. Round-roofed "sow's ear" commuter cars dating from the 1920s were converted into "silk purse" parlor cars, coaches, a diner, and a magnificent, high-windowed observation car at company shops in Indianapolis, Indiana. At the railroad's West Albany (New York) Shops, shrouding was added to the

Against a background of pre-streamliner era heavyweight cars, Gulf, Mobile & Ohio's *Abraham Lincoln*—now more than 30 years old—arrives in Chicago in the summer of 1966. Long before, the train's regal, if austere, blue livery had been replaced by Alton/ GM&O's well-remembered red and maroon.
ALAN L. BRADLEY

ABOVE: New York Central's first crack at streamlining resulted in the *Mercury* streamliner of 1936, designed by industrial stylist Henry Dreyfuss and rebuilt from surplus commuter cars. The railroad promoted the train with a classy folder done in blue and black ink highlighted with silver. The nose of the *Mercury*'s super-streamlined steam locomotive was a prominent element on the folder's cover. MIKE SCHAFER COLLECTION

conventional steam locomotive that had been chosen to power the train. The shrouding melded the locomotive contours with that of the train, but the locomotive's huge driving wheels were left uncovered and—to add visual excitement for trackside onlookers who happened to see the *Mercury* flash by—lighted at night! The *Mercury* was unveiled in 1936.

Designer Henry Dreyfuss—who would two years hence design one of the greatest streamliners ever to roll—was assigned the task of the Cinderella transformation of shabby commuter cars into an avant-garde conveyance. He did it with his trademark "cleanlining" approach to design: simple shapes and trim. Indirect lighting, air-conditioning, sealed windows, carpeting,

The MERCURY

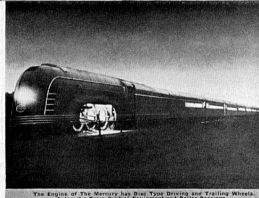

The Engine of The Mercury has Disc Type Driving and Trailing Wheels, Automatic Train Control Equipment and Roller Bearings. Driving Wheels and Rods Illuminated at Night.

Travel in The Mercury train of the New York Central System offers the ultimate in daytime railroad passenger transportation.

The Mercury is a completely air-conditioned, streamlined train which affords the fastest of schedules in either direction between Cleveland, Toledo and Detroit, making the run of 165 miles in 2 hrs. 45 min. westbound and 2 hrs. 50 min. eastbound. The engine of The Mercury is a fast Pacific type streamlined, steam locomotive.

The appointments of The Mercury insure the utmost in comfort. The interiors of each car, including parlor cars, coaches, diners, lounge and observation cars, reflect grace, beauty and modernity of design contributing in a large measure to the popular individuality of The Mercury among the outstanding trains of today.

The Mercury service is used with satisfaction not only by local passengers resident in Cleveland, Toledo or Detroit, but also by travelers from far and wide. The Mercury fits very conveniently into itineraries of those whose missions take them to or through the great cities of The Mercury route. A trip on The Mercury is a real treat.

From its inauguration in the summer of 1936, The Mercury has won the complete and unqualified acceptance of experienced travelers. Why not ride The Mercury on your next trip?

Schedule of The Mercury

(Schedules In Effect September 26, 1937, Subject to Change)
Eastern Standard Time

WESTBOUND TO TOLEDO AND DETROIT

Lv. Cleveland (Cleveland Union Terminal)	7:45 AM
Ar. Toledo (Union Station)	9:25 AM
Lv. Toledo (Union Station)	9:25 AM
Ar. Detroit (Michigan Central Terminal)	10:30 AM

EASTBOUND TO TOLEDO AND CLEVELAND

Lv. Detroit (Michigan Central Terminal)	5:30 PM
Ar. Toledo (Union Station)	6:30 PM
Lv. Toledo (Union Station)	6:30 PM
Ar. Cleveland (Cleveland Union Terminal)	8:20 PM

OTHER TRAINS CLEVELAND TO DETROIT Via New York Central System
Leave Cleveland 12:10 PM; 4:00 PM; 5:35 PM; 12:20 AM; h3:30 AM.

DETROIT TO CLEVELAND
Leave Detroit 8:00 AM; 11:45 AM; h1:25 PM; 8:10 PM; 11:45 PM; 12:30 AM.

h—Indicates arrival at or departure from Erie Railroad Sta., Cleveland

Observation Car of The Mercury

The parlor observation car of The Mercury is an "Observation" car in every sense of the word. The passengers' seats may be turned outward toward the broad windows while in the rounded observation end are two richly upholstered longitudinal settees and a similar lounge facing the rear of the train. Passengers may obtain a full view of the passing scenery. There is a special compartment for checking hand baggage, coats and parcels.

Special Whistle of Musical Tone Distinguishes The Mercury from Other Trains.

Coaches of The Mercury

The streamlined coaches of The Mercury are comfortable and reflect in every way the scheme of the entire train.

The seats are of the double rotating type with movable head rest covers. In the center are four built-in chairs facing each other with table and reading lamps between. The general illumination is indirect.

There is a smoking lounge for men and women equipped with semi-circular settees, loose chairs and tables.

Special attention has been given to the women's dressing room which is extra large, has separate toilet compartment and is fitted with dressing table, illuminated mirror, movable bench and other conveniences contributing to the comfort of women passengers.

Parlor Car of The Mercury

In The Mercury parlor cars are large movable chairs, tables and reading lamps.

The warm colorings of tans, brown, rust and gold provide a restful background.

There is a distinctive and inviting drawing room, accommodating six persons, located midway of the car. There are built-in circular couches, tables, end lamps, coarse weave curtains, folding bridge tables and chairs, all contributing to the unique and pleasant settings.

Hand baggage and coats are cared for in a compartment provided specially for that purpose.

The Floor Plan of Every Car of The Mercury is Individual, Giving the Appearance of a Succession of Rooms.

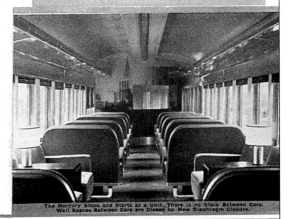

The Mercury Stops and Starts as a Unit. There is no Slack Between Cars. Wall Spaces Between Cars are Closed by New Diaphragm Closure.

and pastels were key elements in transforming the train's interior from the glaring hell on wheels they had been to a glideway of comfort between Detroit and Cleveland.

Enormously successful, additional *Mercury* rolling stock was built and additional trains put in service to Chicago and to Cincinnati. The elderly equipment was finally retired late in the 1950s.

SWIFT OF FOOT: THE HIAWATHA

Even before the New York Central called on its own shop forces to create the *Mercury*, the Chicago, Milwaukee, St. Paul & Pacific—the Milwaukee Road—in 1934 had constructed the first full-sized lightweight passenger car,

No. 4400. Thirty-five percent lighter than a standard railway coach, it also included a number of important new amenities: more space per passenger, reclining seats, air conditioning, wider luggage racks, and larger lavatories and lounges. The 4400 was the brainchild of Karl F. Nystrom, Milwaukee Road's chief mechanical officer, a passenger-car engineering genius who would have a role in creating virtually every streamliner in Milwaukee's future—and there were to be plenty.

Satisfied with the results of its coach experiments and concerned about competition in the Chicago–Minneapolis/St. Paul market thanks to Burlington's new *Twin Zephyr*s, the Milwaukee confidently created the

Hiawatha (named for Longfellow's swift-of-foot hero) right in its own car shops. Introduced on May 29, 1935, the two sets of *Hiawatha* equipment made a splash as the country's first steam-powered lightweight streamliners. In the 1930s, entertainment was where you found it, and thousands flocked to trackside to see the new *Hiawatha*s, which often operated—safely—at speeds of more than 100 MPH. The local press once estimated that if all the spectators observed along the route were placed end-to-end, they would form a line extending from Chicago to a point 75 miles past Minneapolis.

Pulled by a streamlined shrouded steam locomotive, each of the two original trains featured a tap-café whose lounge area was dubbed by Milwaukee Road publicists as the "Tip Top Tap," named for the famous downtown Chicago club lounge of the same name. It housed the first stand-up cocktail bar on any train in America, complete with a handrail so that patrons could steady themselves during the high-speed run between Chicago, Milwaukee, and the Twin Cities. Three coaches offered extra roomy seating and the curved interior of the dining car created a trademark pattern that would be duplicated in subsequent *Hiawatha*s. In contrast to their flashy exterior livery of orange, maroon, and gray with a brown underbody, the cars' interior walls were trimmed in conservative wood grains. But the "Beaver Tail" parlor observation car on the rear was the train's *piece de resistance*. Its broad sloping rear end design minimized wind drag and helped give weight to the *Hiawatha*'s boast that there was "nothing faster on rails" between Chicago and the Twin Cities (despite competition from the same Burlington silver *Zephyr*s that had jump-started the streamliner era in the first place).

The Tip Top Tap lounge of the original *Hiawatha*'s tap-buffet car could seat 24 revelers celebrating the repeal of Prohibition. At the far end of the windowless lounge was the cocktail bar. MILWAUKEE ROAD PHOTO, MILWAUKEE ROAD HISTORICAL ASSOCIATION

The memorable *Hiawatha* styling went beyond the train itself and onto the boarding gates at major *Hiawatha* stations. In this 1936 scene at Chicago Union Station, two sections of the *Hiawatha* are boarding, one on track 15, the other on track 17. MILWAUKEE ROAD PHOTO, MILWAUKEE ROAD HISTORICAL ASSOCIATION

New York Central's 1938-edition *20th Century Limited* speeds along the Hudson River near the Bear Mountain Bridge, New York, in 1938. JAY WILLIAMS COLLECTION

METROPOLITAN PATHWAYS

③

STREAMLINERS LINKING THE EAST COAST WITH MID-AMERICA

Nowhere was the competition for rail passengers greater than over the many railway routes linking East Coast cities and Midwest metropoli—routes that webbed a quadrant of the U.S. that held more than half the country's population. Eight companies vied for travelers pondering transport from the likes of Boston, New York, Washington, and Norfolk over the Appalachians to Chicago, Cincinnati, and St. Louis: the Pennsylvania Railroad, New York Central, Baltimore & Ohio, Chesapeake & Ohio, Norfolk & Western, Erie Railroad, and the Nickel Plate/Lackawanna team. Pennsy and Central were the titans of East Coast–mid-America streamliner operations while the Erie—which never officially launched a fully streamlined train—could barely be counted. The streamliners in this market ranged from the ultra-exclusive *20th Century Limited* between New York and Chicago to Nickel Plate/ Lackawanna's perfunctory *Nickel Plate Limited* and *Westerner/New Yorker*, both of which ran between Chicago and Hoboken, New Jersey.

BELOW: In the only known color photo of PRR's 1938-edition *Liberty Limited*, Raymond Loewy's beautiful "Fleet of Modernism" color scheme glows in late afternoon sun as the train heads out of Chicago's Englewood station in 1939. DAN PETERSON, AL CHIONE COLLECTION COURTESY BOB SCHMIDT

INSET: A colorful brochure introduced Pennsy's newly streamlined "Fleet of Modernism" trains in 1939. JOE WELSH COLLECTION

When rail was the chosen form of public transportation in the U.S., the tracks between the East Coast and mid-America were brimming with an astonishing number and array of passenger trains. Most of them were New York–Chicago trains riding the rails of rivals New York Central (NYC), Pennsylvania Railroad (PRR), and Baltimore & Ohio (B&O).

Streamliners first came to the New York–Chicago market in 1938, and the three top contenders for traffic demonstrated widely varied approaches through their respective chosen designers: Henry Dreyfuss, Raymond Loewy, and Otto Kuhler. The resulting streamliners reflected not only the design concepts of those three individuals, but the railroads themselves.

ULTIMATE RIVALS: THE BROADWAY AND THE CENTURY

Though powerful forces in American transportation, NYC and PRR were conservative while B&O was just plain financially strapped, all three still reeling from the

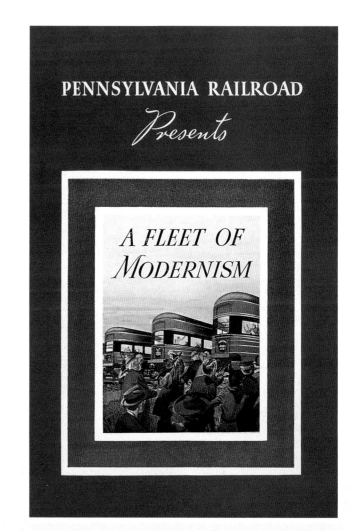

PENNSYLVANIA RAILROAD
Presents

A FLEET OF MODERNISM

Great Depression. Central had frugally, but successfully, experimented with streamliners by building its own: the Detroit–Cleveland *Mercury* of 1936 (chapter 2). Meanwhile, B&O had purchased two new streamliners outright in 1935 for regional service, but soon afterward turned to its own shop forces to produce "new" trains from old rolling stock. The mighty "Pennsy," meanwhile, had little to show save for good intentions of introducing some sort of streamliner. The only concrete result of numerous managerial meetings on the topic was the GG1 electric locomotive, introduced in 1934 and whose carbody design had been "streamstyled" by Raymond Loewy. So, PRR had a streamlined locomotive but no streamlined train when the news broke in 1936 that foe NYC—happy with the results of its *Mercury*—was considering a streamlined rendition of its world-renown *20th Century Limited*, the pride of Central's New York–Chicago "Water Level Route."

PRR officials undoubtedly bristled at the prospect that their world-class New York–Chicago *Broadway Limited*—whose running time, fares, and schedules matched that of the *Century* (both were overnight all-Pullman runs)—might be upstaged. PRR made an unusual move, proposing to NYC that both carriers streamline their premier trains as a joint effort, even to the point of introducing the new trains on the same day. NYC agreed.

Both trains would be built by Pullman-Standard whose parent, the Pullman Company, would own most of the rolling stock, leasing it to PRR and NYC for operation. P-S was an advocate of standardization as a means of cost control, so, from a mechanical and construction standpoint, the cars for both the *Century* and the *Broadway* were essentially identical. Even the floor plans were similar in most of the sleeping cars.

Interestingly, NYC's order for 62 cars would be used to re-equip only its *20th Century Limited*, which because of customer demand routinely ran in two sections (two separate trains operating but a few minutes apart) in each direction, while the PRR's order for 52 cars would not only re-equip the *Broadway*—which normally only ran in one section—but also disperse lightweight, streamlined cars to three other key PRR trains: the New

The colorful environment of a Fleet of Modernism train is captured in this handsome magazine ad from circa 1938. Industrial designer Raymond Loewy's penchant for windowless dining and lounge areas is evident with the couple seated at left, although such arrangements reportedly were unpopular with passengers, most of whom liked to window gaze, even at night. JOE WELSH COLLECTION

RAYMOND LOEWY

Among the numerous styling projects Raymond Loewy tackled for the Pennsylvania Railroad was that of redesigning the carbody of PRR's newly developed GG1-series electric locomotive. Loewy took what had been a clumsy looking, rivet-covered hulk and "streamstyled" it, rounding its contours and applying gold pinstriping that flowed along the locomotive's length, as illustrated by restored GG1 4877 in 1983. JIM BOYD

One of the most prolific industrial designers of the twentieth century, Raymond Loewy is best remembered for his contributions in reshaping the image of the colossal Pennsylvania Railroad. Born in France in 1893, Loewy emigrated to the United States in his mid-twenties in 1919 after serving in the French Army during World War I. With modest engineering training but a great talent for self-promotion, he settled in New York and carved out a successful early career in advertising and fashion illustration. In 1929 came an opportunity to redesign his first machine—the Gestetner Duplicator. Other forays into the new world of industrial design included a relationship with auto manufacturer Hupp Motor Company.

Casting about for new work in the tough times of the Depression, the charming Loewy gained an introduction to Martin Clement, president of the Pennsylvania Railroad—the largest, most-powerful railroad in the U.S. Impressed, Clement recruited Loewy to add style to the railroad's newest electric locomotive design, the GG1. An engineering success, the prototype still suffered from a boxy profile and bristled with unsightly rivets. Loewy conceived a new smooth, welded skin that, together with an attractive paint scheme, made the 79-foot, 238-ton monster look more like a greyhound in flight than a railroad locomotive. PRR eventually operated 139 GG1s. The "G" remained in service for almost 50 years, becoming a household object when the Lionel model train company reproduced it in miniature.

Following the signing of a retainer contract with the railroad in 1935, Loewy's influence could be seen systemwide on everything from locomotives to observation cars, and from stations to waste baskets. He even designed the covers of dining-car menus and the tags for tea bags used on the railroad. Among his most attractive steam-locomotive designs were the experimental S1 and the more successful twin-engine T1 "Duplex." In 1938 Pennsylvania introduced lightweight, streamlined passenger cars to its east–west "Fleet of Modernism." Loewy styled both the exteriors and interiors of the cars. After World War II, Loewy continued his relationship with the PRR, completing the design of a new series of passenger cars, which included such innovations as a recreation car with a playroom for children and a newsreel theater. As costs rose and revenues dropped, the passenger train—and, for that matter, the Pennsylvania Railroad—went into a long, irreversible decline. The Pennsy and Raymond Loewy went their separate ways in 1952.

Nevertheless, the great designer continued to shape our everyday life. Loewy provided design consulting for Coca-Cola, United Airlines, and IBM to name a few. He created the timeless paint scheme still in use on Air Force One and even broke the bonds of earth, assisting in the design of Skylab for NASA. His autobiography was appropriately entitled: *Never Leave Well Enough Alone.* Feisty to the end, Raymond Loewy, an American (and French) genius died in 1986 at the age of 93.

York–Chicago *General*, the New York–St. Louis *"Spirit of St. Louis,"* and the Chicago–Washington *Liberty Limited.* In applying its streamlining efforts to more than just the *Broadway*, PRR developed a marketing ploy that spotlighted several trains as the "Fleet of Modernism."

From an art standpoint, the locomotives and cars for the *Century* and the *Broadway*—since they were mechanically nearly identical—could be considered as blank canvases on which two different artists—Loewy for Pennsy, Dreyfuss for Central—would work their magic in terms of exterior cloaking and interior décor. The results were striking—and polarized. In their newly streamlined incarnation, the two trains emerged with two distinctive personalities. The new *20th Century Limited* and the *Broadway* (and its Modernism sisters) were launched on June 6, 1938.

The *Broadway Limited* had been an institution on the Pennsylvania's New York–Philadelphia–Pittsburgh–Chicago route since 1902, providing first-class-only service to Philadelphia and Chicago bankers and New York Wall Streeters who knew the sprawling PRR as the most-powerful railroad in North America.

The typical makeup for the newly streamlined *Broadway Limited* included a baggage-mail car; a bar-lounge sleeper with secretary's room, shower bath, and barber shop; four sleeping cars with various room configurations for one to four people; dining car; and a buffet-lounge sleeper-observation car. All but the baggage-mail and diner were built new by Pullman-Standard; these two 1920s-era heavyweight cars were modernized by PRR's Altoona (Pennsylvania) Shops.

Powering this typical equipment set between Pennsylvania Station in Manhattan and the end of PRR's electrified district at Harrisburg, Pennsylvania, was one of PRR's famous Raymond Loewy-styled GG1-series electric locomotives (sidebar). Beyond to Chicago, a Pacific-type steam locomotive rebuilt with streamlined shrouding often handled the train.

Tuscan red, a hue that had already become closely associated with the PRR, was the key color on the exterior of Fleet of Modernism cars, offset by a maroon window band that was rounded toward the car ends—a somewhat radical treatment where protocol usually called for a linear, continuous design that made coupled railcars appear as one long unit. Gold pinstriping provided the Art Deco touch and emphasized modernity.

Loewy's palette was even more colorful when it came to designing car interiors. He strove for cheeriness through eye-catching color combinations, employing various shades of red, yellow, orange, blue, black, and white, sometimes with metallic accents and a generous, tasteful use of rare-wood veneers. Some of Loewy's lounge and dining-car arrangements were perhaps controversial, as he had a penchant for isolating passengers from the outside world with long stretches of walls featuring, instead of windows, cork panels or murals depicting transportation themes. Perhaps the idea was that, since most of the *Broadway*'s travel occurred during hours of darkness, lounge-car revelers would be looking at each other and not out into the inky blackness of night in the Appalachian Mountains. Apparently this did not appeal to the claustrophobically inclined, as the windowless seats reportedly were always the last to fill up.

In the dining car, a windowless section in the middle of the dining area, set off by narrow dividers, featured inward-facing banquettes seating four. At the far end of the dining area, curved glass partitions set aside a small lounge area with a walnut bar. The dining car featured a telephone system whereby patrons could call from their sleeper or a lounge car to check on seating availability or make dinner reservations.

Fleet of Modernism–themed scenes adorned Pennsylvania Railroad public passenger timetables of the period. This 1939 timetable illustrated a diner interior, while inside, the timetable featured the "Dining Out on the Fleet of Modernism" ad shown on page 43.

The signature vehicles of both the *Century* and *Broadway* were the sleeper-lounge observation cars at train's end. In the two *Broadway* cars, named *Metropolitan View* and *Skyline View*, Loewy created two adjacent lounge areas featuring curved end walls and oval seating areas. Situated at the very end of the car, the observation lounge featured three sets of love seats arranged for outward viewing. Upper walls painted in rose-tan lacquer reached to curved ceilings clad in copper lacquer that were illuminated by indirect lighting. Blue was a keynote color in easy chairs, tables (capped with the new Formica covering that was becoming all the rage in American life), carpeting, curtains, and wainscoting while the lounge sofas were covered in brown leather. Venetian blinds—*de riguer* on early streamliners—adorned nearly all windows.

WHETHER IT WAS New York Central's intention to create the ultimate passenger train when it decided to streamline its *20th Century Limited*—which had been providing impeccable service since 1902—is anybody's guess, but arguably that's what happened. Transportation historians consistently rate the 1938 edition of the *Century* to be the world's ultimate passenger conveyance—at least on the ground. (Oceanliner aficionados might have good cause to dispute this point.)

Much of the success of the *Century's* design execution can be attributed to Central's chosen industrial-design wizard, Henry Dreyfuss, one of the most influential modern-era designers of the period. Dreyfuss's approach to design was known as "cleanlining," wherein design elements were reduced to their most basic forms—a hallmark of the growing *moderne* movement. The Dreyfuss touch had already marked the *Mercury*, and in 1936 he brought the *Century*—from locomotive to napkin holders—to his drawing board.

The steam locomotives regularly assigned to the new *20th Century Limited* west of Harmon, New York (boxy electric locomotives shuttled the train between subterranean Grand Central Terminal and Harmon station outside New York City) were the epitome of streamlined steam. The Dreyfuss styling as applied to these locomotives became an icon of not only the New York Central Railroad but of train streamlining in general, and the distinct contours of these long-ago-scrapped locomotives still show up in the public eye, incorporated into retro designs that recall the Art Deco age.

The Dreyfuss Hudson locomotive featured a bullet nose accented with a satin-finish aluminum fin suggestive of a Roman gladiator helmet. In stark contrast to streamlined steam locomotive No. 3768 assigned (somewhat sporadically) to Pennsy's *Broadway*, the driving rods and wheels of the Central's locomotives were completely visible, allowing trackside spectators to witness the dynamics of steam locomotion at its best. (Pennsy's locomotive was so completely shrouded that the running gear was almost entirely covered.) *Century* locomotive tenders were contoured to match the passenger cars that trailed behind them, and together the locomotive and tender were painted to match the cars: light gray and a dark gray band (starting on the tender) with aluminum-colored center stripes and Opex blue separation stripes. (PRR's No. 3768 was a dark gunmetal color while the GG1 electric locomotives initially were Brunswick green; both locomotive types were handsomely painted, but curiously they weren't decorated to match the two-tone Tuscan red Fleet of Modernism colors in any way other than gold-pinstriping.)

The typical makeup for the main section of the *20th Century Limited* included a mail-baggage car, dormitory-buffet-lounge car, five sleeping cars, two dining cars, two more sleepers, and a sleeper-lounge observation car. The four buffet-lounge cars in the pool carried the names *Century Club*, *Century Lounge*, *Century Inn*, and *Century Tavern*. In addition to the buffet-lounge, these cars also

Dreyfuss styled just about every aspect of the 1938 *20th Century Limited*, from its 100 MPH Hudson-type steam locomotives down to its fine dining-car crockery. The simple "cleanlining" approach (and Dreyfuss's apparent attachment to gray) to the whole train is evident in this dinner plate. REPRODUCTION PLATE FROM PRIVATE CAR LIMITED, BELLEVILLE, ILLINOIS

HENRY DREYFUSS

When *Time* Magazine chose one all-inclusive icon to represent the twentieth century, it picked the steam locomotive designed for the 1938 *20th Century Limited* by Henry Dreyfuss (1904–1972). In fact, many Dreyfuss creations could be included on a "most memorable but unsung" list, including Bell telephones of 1937, 1949, and the Trimline phone of 1965; the round Honeywell thermostat; and John Deere's "New Generation of Power" tractors of the 1960s, with seats redesigned to please farmers.

Benefitting from experience he gained creating theatrical sets in the 1920s, Dreyfuss was one of the first industrial designers to effectively integrate the human dimension into industrial design. His creative contributions to the New York Central dated from the early 1930s, when he met with NYC officials in New York to submit a design for a new streamliner. The railroad rejected his proposal as being too expensive. On his way home from the meeting, Dreyfuss noticed dozens of surplus commuter coaches sitting idle in the railroad's Mott Haven yard. His suggestion to rebuild the cars became the catalyst for the Detroit–Cleveland *Mercury* steam-powered streamliner and precursor to two Dreyfuss masterpieces, the *20th Century Limited*s of 1938 and 1948.

The 1938 *Century*'s silver-maned, skirted locomotive and tender, contoured to match the trailing cars, were linear styling breakthroughs. Inside, all the designer's ingenuity was brought into play to break the long tunnel effect inherent in railcar interiors. By repeating the type style, logo, striping and color scheme on stationery, dinner china, and even matchbooks, he created an instantly recognizeable "branding" for the *Century*. Yet his success with the *20th Century Limited* was just a tiny part of the contribution Henry Dreyfuss made to the world of industrial design.

Henry Dreyfuss will forever be associated with the 1938 *20th Century Limited*, identified by its knife-prow Hudson-type steam locomotives, here lined up on the cover of the brochure announcing the train. JOE WELSH COLLECTION

A subdued interior for exciting people: In the observation car of the 1938 *20th Century Limited*, Henry Dreyfuss utilized cool blues and grays to suggest exclusivity and sophistication, accented with walnut and pigskin colors in selected seating. This oil illustration shows the forward end of the car as viewed from the observation area. ILLUSTRATION BY MITCH MARKOVITZ

featured a barber shop—a statement on NYC's exceptionally smooth Water Level Route main line. Upon entering the car, passengers passed through a curved-wall foyer that displayed models of early NYC steam locomotives. In the lounge area, Dreyfuss grouped the seating—comprised of both settees and individual chairs, all done in leather—and arranged it to break up the "tunnel effect" so common in rail passenger cars, even today.

The *Century*'s diners were on par with any fine Manhattan restaurant in terms of décor as well as food quality. Again, Dreyfuss sought to alleviate the tunnel effect, dividing dining areas with partially glassed wall partitions. The main dining room seated 22 and was flanked by two intimate "dinette" areas, each seating eight at two tables. Seating was in the form of settees and traditional individual chairs arranged around tables of varying shapes and sizes and either perpendicular or parallel to the walls and windows, thus avoiding the predictable lockstep table arrangement found in most dining cars.

The *Century*'s diners were dual-purpose. After the dinner hour, crewmembers cleared the tables of white linens, replacing them with rust-colored tablecloths; the room lights were supplanted with soft, rosy indirect lighting. Music was the final touch in this transformation of what had been the *Century*'s "restaurant" into an elegant night club known as "Café Century."

Each of the four sleeper-lounge observation cars in the *Century* pool—*Manhattan Island, Pelee Island, Bedloes Island*, and *Thousand Islands*—featured a master room and an adjacent double bedroom, but the rest of the car was devoted to a stunning lounge. The main lounge area was set off by two bulkheads featuring two photomurals, one with the Manhattan skyline and the opposite featuring Chicago. Floor-to-ceiling gunmetal gray columnar supports along the walls imparted a citified atmosphere while passively partitioning seated guests into groups (a Dreyfuss hallmark). Walls were covered in gray leather; the settee seating, in blue. Moveable individual seats were upholstered with leather of a color referred to, perhaps unceremoniously, as "pigskin." The solarium (observation area) end featured curved blue-leather settees that faced outward, allowing patrons to watch the constantly receding scenery. A bulkhead divider featuring a map of the NYC, a model of an NYC *Century* Hudson locomotive, and a working speedometer set the solarium area apart from the main lounge.

The designs of the *Broadway* and *Century* sleeping cars was fairly standardized, but the designs of the feature cars—the diners, lounge cars, and sleeper-lounge observations cars—served to set each train apart.

That such markedly diverse personalities could emerge from two trains that, mechanically, were nearly identical and marketed to society's upper echelon is testament to the impact and importance of environmental design. The 1938 *Broadway* was warm, colorful, and cheery, yet the bold, modernistic interior said "style, strength, and industry." And it said "Pennsylvania Railroad," which was entirely intended. It was a train used by old-money society. The train itself was the star.

The *Century*'s design was spectacularly understated, and it said one thing: "New York exclusivity." From the moment you stepped aboard, you knew you had arrived, for the *Century* catered to the new-money elite of New York and Chicago: movie and stage personalities and successful business people who had achieved. The *Century*'s low-key but sophisticated surroundings allowed the passengers to be the stars.

Which of these two new streamliners was the best? Passenger-train historians will forever argue the merits of either train, but ridership statistics do seem to reveal a preference. The *Broadway* suffered from low ridership following its 1938 streamlining, while the *20th Century Limited* routinely ran in two or more sections to accommodate demand. Yet, in an ironic twist, the *Century* was discontinued in 1967 while the *Broadway* would soldier on in one form or another for nearly 30 more years.

B&O'S CAPITOL IDEA

Although Baltimore & Ohio was America's first common-carrier railroad and the first American railroad to offer scheduled passenger service, the venerable carrier was nonetheless one of the underdogs—but the strongest one—in the East Coast–mid-America market. Hampered by lack of a direct entrance into Manhattan,

An exciting interior for subdued people: A rendering of the sleeper-buffet-lounge observation car of PRR's 1938 *Broadway Limited* illustrates Loewy's unbridled yet competent use of the color spectrum. The view looks rearward from the main lounge area toward the solarium (observation) end of the car.
ILLUSTRATION BY MITCH MARKOVITZ

hattan, a roundabout route west of New York that passed through Washington, D.C. and over rugged Appalachian grades, and severe financial constraints owing to the Great Depression, B&O's efforts at streamlining were of more practical nature yet notable in their own right.

B&O's answer to NYC's and PRR's premier overnight all-Pullman trains between New York and Chicago was the *Capitol Limited*, a latecomer to the East Coast–Chicago market, having been inaugurated in 1923. Significantly, B&O was one of the first railroads to purchase brand-new streamliners (chapter 2) when it introduced the short-haul Jersey City–Washington *Royal Blue* in 1935. Apparently unsatisfied with the new equipment, though, B&O reverted to the tried-and-true heavyweight passenger car for its next efforts at streamlining. Calling on the skilled workers at its Mount Clare Shops in Baltimore as well as at Pullman-Standard, B&O had dozens of standard cars rebuilt into modern streamlined (though not lightweight) equipment—at a fraction of the cost of buying new equipment. Thus, the first streamlined *Capitol Limited*, inaugurated in 1938—the same year as the newly streamlined *Century* and *Broadway* were launched—featured an altogether different look and feel.

Like Central and Pennsy, the B&O hired an industrial designer for the project, selecting Otto Kuhler—a man destined to become synonymous with designwork throughout the railroad industry. Under Kuhler's direction, the new *Capitol Limited* took on a regal splendor befitting a train that was in effect an ambassador to the nation's capital, since most of its business was Washington-oriented.

Most of Kuhler's touches were on the outside of the train. In the rebuilding process, the heavyweight cars chosen for the upgraded *Capitol* had their clerestory roofs replaced with rounded roofs—a process that did more to

Pullman Observation Lounge — a pleasant place to relax, read and view the scenery

Passengers enjoy the special convenience of the private bedr

Club-like appointments in the Buffet-Coach Lounge

A social hour in the Observation Lounge

Every modern convenience in these restful, Individual Reclining Seat Coaches

A large promotional folder, shown about half original size, introduced not only the modernized *Capitol Limited* but its Jersey City–Washington–St. Louis cousin, the *National Limited*. Compared to the *Broadway* and the *Century*, the B&O streamliners had a more dated, traditional look (except for their new diesels). WILLIAM HOWES JR. COLLECTION

enhance a streamlining effect than anything else. Although the cars retained their decidedly unstreamlined vertical rectangular windows so typical of standard-era passenger cars, the addition of full skirting and full-width diaphragms (coverings between cars) further added to the streamlining effect.

The most radical difference between the new *Capitol Limited* and its peers involved its locomotives. Powering

ENJOY...
Extra Travel Comfort
on B & O's DIESEL-POWER STREAMLINERS
to the *East!*

YES, a ticket on either of these popular trains—the CAPITOL LIMITED or the NATIONAL LIMITED—calls for more than just a train ride. Every railroad provides that! It's the host of *extras* in comforts, appointments and conveniences that means so much to Pullman and Coach passengers who prefer the "Route of the Diesel-power Streamliners"!

EXTRA COMFORT WITH DIESEL-POWER

Diesel-Power, for example! As modern as today! As smooth-riding as a glide thru space! No annoying changes of engines en route. Nothing to disturb sleep or rest. And besides, both trains are equipped with rubber draft gear to lessen jolts, and rubber-cushioned trucks and underframes to reduce vibration. Quiet, restful and comfortable! Speed and safety in a setting that offers the highest standard of railroad service. No other trains from Chicago or St. Louis to the East offer so many inviting comforts!

FOR PULLMAN PASSENGERS

There are Private Bedrooms, Drawing Rooms, Compartments and regular Sections. Dining Cars. Sunroom-Observation Lounge cars, with roomy, movable chairs; writing desks, stationery and current mag-azines; Radio and Valet. In addition, on the CAPITOL LIMITED: Train Secretary to take dictation (at no cost) and Maid-Manicure. On the NATIONAL LIMITED: Stewardess-Registered-Nurse service for Pullman and Coach passengers, without charge. Especially helpful to women and children and to elderly folks.

FOR COACH PASSENGERS

Individual Reclining Seat Coaches, beautifully furnished and decorated with soft, mellow lights; wide, deep-cushioned individual seats, with foot rests, linen head rests and seat-backs adjustable to almost any angle for comfort. Women's Rest Rooms are fitted in the modern manner, with large settee, chair, smoking stand, mirror with tubular lights, double wash basin and lavatory. Soft, downy pillows at nominal cost. Coach Seats reserved *free* for thru passengers, in advance, if desired.

NEW-STYLE BUFFET-COACH-LOUNGE

Each train features a new style Buffet-Coach-Lounge equipped with big, easy chairs for rest and relaxation, card tables and a Radio. The modern Buffet serves beverages, sandwiches, light lunches and full meals, at popular prices. Coach passengers may enjoy all of these Club Car conveniences at no extra cost.

· · · **BOTH TRAINS DIESEL-POWERED TO WASHINGTON** · · ·

Women's Rest Rooms in the Coaches offer many unusual comforts

Stewardess - Registered Nurse — a helpful, personal service on the National Limited

Attractive Dining Cars— serving delicious B & O meals, reasonably-priced

Train Secretary on the Capitol Limited takes dictation and does typing — without charge

Radio entertainment for Coach and Pullman passengers

---

the new *Capitol Limited* were brand-new Electro-Motive EA/EB-series diesel-electric passenger units, making the *Capitol* among the first passenger trains to employ independent "catalog" locomotives—that is, off-the-shelf diesel-electrics that could be assigned to just about any passenger train, not necessarily the *Capitol*, although that and the Jersey City–St. Louis *National Limited* were the locomotives' initial assignments.

Kuhler devised a noble exterior color scheme of royal blue (already synonymous with the B&O) and gray offset by gold striping and lettering. The locomotives were similarly attired, but with a black stripe in addition to the blue and gray banding. Such would serve as the signature color scheme of the B&O for the next quarter century, and today railroad historians rank it one of the most outstanding classic railroad paint schemes.

OTTO KUHLER

One of German-born industrial designer Otto Kuhler's great avocations was painting, drawing, or etching dramatic scenes of bulky steam locomotives. His subject may have been Seaboard's heavyweight *Orange Blossom Special* (which ultimately was never streamlined) "at speed" or a series of dramatic still lifes sketched near roundhouses between 1928 and 1930 with titles such as "Giants on Call," "Panting Brute," and "Rattler." But soon Kuhler was asked to try his hand at something "full-sized industrial"—a steam locomotive and its passenger train. Starting with his inspiring design of the Milwaukee Road's *Hiawatha* of 1935, Kuhler became adept at creating the image of speed on bulky or unconventional rolling stock. He developed the color scheme and striping for the Gulf, Mobile & Northern's *Rebels* of 1935, then followed up the job on that smallish articulated streamliner with the restyling of Baltimore & Ohio's *Royal Blue* heavyweight cars of 1937 as well some of the interior design and exterior paint scheme of B&O's *Capitol Limited* and *National Limited* of 1938. In 1939–40 he designed Lehigh Valley's *Asa Packer*, *John Wilkes*, and *Black Diamond*—also heavyweight steam-powered trains in streamliner dress. In 1940, it was back to streamstyling a steam engine for a Rock Island *Rocket* and designing a new red-and-silver look for Gulf, Mobile & Ohio's heavyweight *Gulf Coast Rebel*, a masterful use of paint and converging lines. But Kuhler never lost his touch with the brush. "Few printmakers conveyed the scale and sheer force of the modern locomotive better than Otto Kuhler," explains Kevin Sharp, Curator of American Art at the Norton Museum. And unlike other artists who might have titled a 1935 painting, "*Hiawatha* at Night," Kuhler had more than a passing involvement in the subject.

The new Electro-Motive E-series diesel-electric passenger locomotives assigned to the newly streamlined *Capitol Limited* and *National Limited* in 1938 were clad in a regal paint scheme developed by Otto Kuhler. He chose a combination of blue, black, and gray separated by yellow pinstriping. This livery was applied to passenger rolling stock and, later, freight locomotives as well. EMD

The coach-buffet-lounge of the newly streamlined *National Limited* of 1940 featured inlaid tile flooring, tubular metalwork, and indirect lighting, influenced by designer Otto Kuhler. BILL HOWES COLLECTION

A regular 1938 *Capitol Limited* consist included nine cars: a baggage-dormitory-club car, six sleepers, diner, and a sleeper-lounge observation car with a sun room. Kuhler held back on radical interior design. Rather than either the low-key but futuristic look adopted by NYC or the bold, modern appearance within PRR's Fleet of Modernism, Kuhler employed only a modest dose of Art Deco through light wall and ceiling colors, furniture with tubular chrome frames, and indirect lighting. And yet, "retro" was the key to B&O dining cars. For the revamped *Capitol*, B&O selected some of its 1920s-era diners that had a Colonial motif. Although these cars received the same new exterior treatment as the rest, the Colonial décor was retained, possibly because B&O dining service had long been held in high regard and the Colonial diners had become closely associated with superior dining fare and service. George and Martha Washington would have felt right at home.

In 1940, B&O's *National Limited* was similarly upgraded, with heavyweight cars rebuilt by Pullman and B&O's Mount Clare Shops. Again, the Kuhler touch was evident, and the extent of modernization was greater on car interiors than it had been on the *Capitol*.

AFTER THE WAR

World War II was a turning point for many things, including streamliner design. By this time, the Art Deco movement had been tempered, with futurism yielding to the smart, sophisticated *moderne* movement. The overall design theme had gone from looking toward the future to *being* in the future. However, practicality had entered into the equation more than ever. In the years immediately following World War II, railroads embarked upon an unprecedented move to streamline or otherwise upgrade their passenger-train fleets. Prior to the war, many streamliners, as we have seen, were custom-designed from top to bottom. Following the war, this approach became less practical. Instead of just one or two

select trains being streamlined, some railroads were modernizing whole fleets. Consequently, many of the new trains (or new editions of existing streamliners) comprised "off-the-shelf" locomotives and rolling stock, often designed in-house by the car or locomotive manufacturer or as directed by a railroad's mechanical and marketing departments. Such was often the case for the east-west carriers featured in this chapter.

In 1948–49, the *Broadway* and *Century* were again re-equipped, and again their respective designers were called upon to orchestrate each train's new appearance. However, PRR, NYC, and B&O at the same time ordered new locomotives and passenger cars for many other trains as well. The extent to which Henry Dreyfuss, Raymond Loewy, and Otto Kuhler extended their design influence on all the newly streamlined trains during this frenetic postwar period is unclear. Quite likely, the railroads ordered carbuilders to simply adopt much of the design established by these designers prior to the war.

The 1948–49 *Broadway* and *Century* certainly bore the marks of Loewy and Dreyfuss, though the Art Deco

FASTER than ever
BETTER than ever

THE GENERAL

NEW YORK–CHICAGO
16 HOURS

FEATURING NEW ALL-PRIVATE-ROOM SLEEPING CARS

BELOW: In the face of dieselization, the Pennsylvania Railroad attempted to carry on the evolution of heavy-duty, high-speed steam locomotion. The resulting 52 war-baby "Duplex" T-1 steam locomotives bore rakish "sharknose" styling developed by Raymond Loewy. At the Englewood station stop near Chicago in 1946, a T-1 heads up the *General*. J. R. QUINN

INSET: Cover of brochure announcing Pennsy's 1948–49 upgrading and re-equipping of its New York–Chicago *General*. JOE WELSH COLLECTION

look that was so strong in the 1938 *Century* had been toned down. Yet, such elements as the rust, tan, and blue interior colors of the 1938 train prevailed on the 1948 edition. One of the most significant changes involved the *Century's* exterior paint scheme, which was now dark gray with a light-gray window band edged in aluminum-white. New E-series passenger diesels manufactured by General Motors' Electro-Motive Division and clad in an EMD-designed "lightning stripe" scheme had replaced the unforgettable streamlined Hudson steam locomotives, which had fallen victim to the dieselization movement that was sweeping through American railroads.

The postwar period saw a dramatic rise in coach-class rail travel, and railroads responded with new streamliners aimed at this economy-minded market. Among the best-known coach streamliners in the East Coast–Midwest market were New York Central's *Pacemaker* (New York–Chicago) and *Empire State Express* (New York–Buffalo–Cleveland), Pennsylvania's *Trail Blazer* (New York–Chicago) and *Jeffersonian* (New York–St. Louis), Baltimore & Ohio's *Columbian* (Washington–Chicago), and

A stylish folder showed—with a bit of exaggeration in terms of the standard railcar width of 10 feet—accommodations aboard the newly re-equipped *Broadway Limited* of 1948–49.
MIKE SCHAFER COLLECTION

The New
BROADWAY LIMITED
NEW YORK • CHICAGO
Now in Service

MASTER ROOMS—Extra-spacious for two! Radio . . . four comfortable folding lounge chairs . . . two full-size beds lower from the wall at night. As in all rooms—lighting, heating and air-conditioning are individually controlled to your preference. Enclosed toilet facilities including *shower bath*.

NEW MID-TRAIN LOUNGE AND OBSERVATION LOUNGE CARS—Cheerful, spacious settings—richly appointed for leisure with deep, soft carpets . . . roomy settees . . . richly-upholstered arm chairs. Latest periodicals are in the libraries. Convenient buffets provide a wide choice of refreshments.

NEW MASTER DINING CAR—so attractively decorated . . . spacious! Enjoy delicious food . . . meticulous service . . . distinctive table appointments . . . the *Broadway Limited's* traditional touch at mealtime. Separate, new kitchen car is adjoining—thus more table space . . . more comfort for dining.

DRAWING ROOMS—with complete facilities for three persons. Restful sofa and two folding easy chairs are replaced at night by the three beds shown above. Two wide windows . . . extra-large wardrobe . . . ample dressing space . . . enclosed toilet annex.

COMPARTMENTS have been re-designed to afford extra privacy for two persons. During the day—a wide sofa-seat and folding lounge chair. For slumber hours—easily accessible lower and upper beds. Full-length wardrobe . . . enclosed toilet annex.

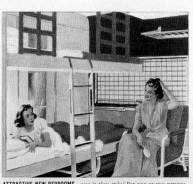

ATTRACTIVE NEW BEDROOMS—*now in three styles!* For one or two persons, each has its own comfortable arrangement by day. Slumber-inviting lower and upper beds . . . full-length wardrobe . . . enclosed toilet annex. Adjoining Bedrooms may be purchased en suite and converted to one large room.

DUPLEX ROOMS—an upstairs-or-downstairs room—*something new* for the individual on the *Broadway Limited*. Full-length bed at night—a roomy daytime sofa. Handy writing table . . . complete toilet facilities.

NOW MORE OF THE POPULAR ROOMETTES—completely private for one person's comfort. An easy turn of a lever lowers your bed from the wall, replacing the restful daytime sofa-seat shown above. Enclosed wardrobe . . . panorama window . . . complete toilet facilities.

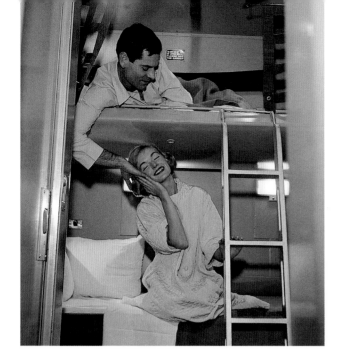

ABOVE: As inhibitions began to fall by the wayside after World War II, advertising began to take on stronger sexual undertones throughout America. Always notoriously conservative, American railroads even yielded to romance to sell their services. In this classic 1950s publicity photo, New York Central suggested more than a good night's sleep on its *20th Century Limited* and other east–west trains (although the bunk beds perhaps helped tone down any inferences). ED NOWAK/NEW YORK CENTRAL SYSTEM, COURTESY ROBERT YANOSEY, MORNING SUN BOOKS

Norfolk & Western's *Powhatan Arrow* (Norfolk–Cincinnati). The *Pacemaker* had been implemented between New York and Chicago during the war using rebuilt rolling stock quite similar to that of the *Mercury*, but when NYC embarked on is massive train-upgrading program in the late 1940s, the *Pacemaker* received all-new stainless-steel cars from the Budd Company. Nearly the same scenario applied to PRR's *Trail Blazer* and B&O's *Columbian*. Advertising for the *Pacemaker* was aimed at the budget-conscious yet cosmopolitan traveler.

The postwar *Columbian* was B&O's first all-new streamliner since its *Abraham Lincoln* and *Royal Blue* trains of 1935. Pullman-Standard delivered two eight-car sets of *Columbian* equipment (each train had a baggage-

Chicago's Board of Trade building stands prominently in a cityscape then bereft of the mega-skyscrapers that populate the Loop area today as the *20th Century Limited* homes in on La Salle Street Station on September 1, 1962. Note the two tykes playing kissy face in the rear window. This is the 1948—and last—edition of the *Century*, with its dark gray paint scheme that would become standard on many of NYC's smooth-sided passenger cars after World War II. BOB JOHNSTON

New CLUB CAR *luxury... designed for living*

TWO CLUB CARS The *Pacemaker* carries a smart mid-train lounge adjoining the dining car and a spacious observation car.

LAZE AND GAZE Stroll back to the streamlined observation car for a change of scene, music, before meal time refreshments, a quiet game or chat . . . or relax and enjoy the endless fascination of lazing in the glassed-in observation compartment while gazing at America through wide, rear-view windows . . . along the scenic Water Level Route.

ABOVE: New York Central's *Pacemaker* was launched in 1939 using upgraded heavyweight cars. Ten years later, it was completely re-equipped with brand-new lightweight, streamlined cars built by the Budd Company. A brochure issued for the 1949 train provided an interesting cutaway view of the *Pacemaker*'s tavern-lounge observation car as well as a rendering of the lounge section of the train's kitchen-lounge car, which operated adjacent to a full dining car. KEVIN HOLLAND COLLECTION

RIGHT: The conductor of the *Empire State Express* reviews the coach-seat reservation diagram with the train stewardess before collecting tickets. Approximately 40 original mural paintings depicting historical scenes along NYC's Water Level Route were created for the train. The interior colors of coral peach (walls) and blue-green (upholstery) were a prewar classic. The train's inauguration on December 7, 1941, was tempered by much larger news: the attack on Pearl Harbor. ILLUSTRATION BY MITCH MARKOVITZ

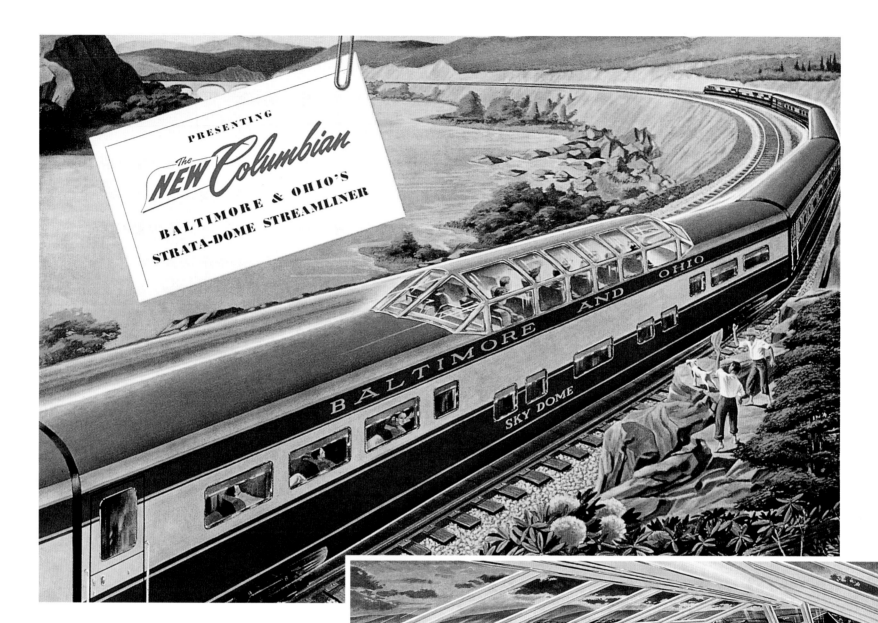

PRESENTING
The NEW Columbian
BALTIMORE & OHIO'S
STRATA-DOME STREAMLINER

BALTIMORE AND OHIO

SKY DOME

ABOVE: The debut of Baltimore & Ohio's newly streamlined *Columbian* was a highly publicized event that included the issuance of a lavish 16-page brochure, the cover of which is shown approximately 75 percent of actual size. B&O was particularly proud of the train's Strata-Dome coach, prominentaly featured on the cover illustration (with the "people waving at the train" format so popular before the era of trackside rock-pelting hooligans). Inside the brochure (RIGHT), artist Lauren Smith provided a detailed view of the dome interior. The first dome cars in the East, B&O's Strata-Dome coaches sported speedometers, altimeters, and barometers. KEVIN J. HOLLAND COLLECTION

dormitory-lounge car, four coaches, a dome coach, diner, and lounge observation car) in 1949. Clad in the classic Kuhler-inspired blue-and-gray livery, but with interiors designed in-house at least in part by P-S, the *Columbian* elicited much promotion from parent B&O. Like many new postwar trains, interior design strove for the contemporary rather than future, with an eye on cheerful décor using combinations of blue and wine red trimmed with stainless steel. Wood paneling in the lounge observation car and Venetian blinds throughout provided a homey touch while angled, legless table seating (the tables were cantilevered from the walls) in the carpeted dining car conveyed the feel of a fine hotel restaurant. Women's lounges offered full-length mirrors, satin-finished chrome, and blue Marbelle flooring.

The *Columbian*'s most exceptional vehicle was the Strata-Dome car, a postwar innovation—upper-level seating under a glass dome—that was quickly becoming popularized on many Midwestern regional streamliners and Western transcontinental trains. The *Columbian* was the first East Coast–Midwest streamliner to feature such a car, and B&O promoted it heavily. (Tight clearances at the Manhattan stations of PRR and NYC prevented them from ever purchasing dome cars.)

Meanwhile, B&O's esteemed all-Pullman *Capitol Limited* and Jersey City–Washington–St. Louis *National Limited* were in the midst of a more gradual upgrading with new lightweight sleeping cars. As with the *Columbian* and *Capitol Limited,* the *National* initially had been streamlined with heavyweight equipment modernized by Pullman and B&O's Mount Clare Shops. In an interesting twist, the *Capitol* and *National* were further upgraded in the late 1950s with lightweight, streamlined cars purchased secondhand from New York Central and Chesapeake & Ohio, with the interior décor that had been employed by those carriers left largely intact. By this time, passenger revenues were declining nationwide, and railroads had much more to worry about that maintaining uniform, by-the-train interior décors in their streamliners. Instead, cars were often "pooled" and thus made available for service on any train, regardless of which train they may have been built for.

The *National Limited* was the star of Baltimore & Ohio's Jersey City– Washington–Cincinnati–St. Louis route. With a mixture of new cars built by Pullman-Standard and older, heavyweight cars modernized by B&O's Mount Clare Shops, the *National* is shown sweeping across ancient Thomas Viaduct at Relay, Maryland, in the spring of 1965. Even in its twilight years, the *National* still maintained a regal look in its Otto Kuhler-inspired blue-and-gray livery. At train's end is a sleeper-lounge observation car originally built for the New York Central. BOB JOHNSTON

Overshadowed by titans New York Central, Pennsylvania, and, to a lesser degree Baltimore & Ohio, east-west carriers Chesapeake & Ohio, Norfolk & Western, and the Nickel Plate–Lackawanna Railroad amalgamation nonetheless joined the streamliner bandwagon.

Chesapeake & Ohio operated a rather substantial network of passenger trains between Washington, D.C., the Virginia coast, Cincinnati, Louisville, and Detroit but didn't even dabble in streamlining until after World War II. Then it did so in a big way by ordering 46 cars from the Budd Company for a spectacular day domeliner between Washington and Cincinnati (with split-off sections serving Newport News, Virginia, and Louisville) that was to be known as *The Chessie,* named for C&O's famous feline mascot.

C&O people collaborated with designers at the Budd Company as well as Baldwin Locomotive Works on the design of the train and its special steam turbine-electric locomotives. The results were extraordinary. Every coach had a lounge area and luggage lockers, while the "Family Coaches" featured playrooms for children. The train's social center—the tavern-lounge cars—each contained an illuminated aquarium and interior colors that enhanced the marine theme: aquamarine, vermilion, and yellow. (Unfortunately, the fish in the aquarium died of motion sickness when the tavern-lounge cars finally entered service.) Each trainset's twin-unit food-service car sets featured a kitchen, lunch counter, and full dining room. After dinner, the diner was to be converted to a movie theater.

All three sets of *Chessie* equipment arrived in 1948—just as the *Chessie* project was quietly terminated by the railroad for economic reasons. Although the shiny new stainless-steel rolling stock had been delivered complete with orange letterboards carrying the train's name, none of the cars ever operated unified as *The Chessie.* C&O kept a few cars to upgrade its existing trains while the rest were sold to other railroads. C&O concentrated its ensuing streamlining efforts on its existing Washington- and Tidewater-to-the-Midwest runs: the *George Washington, F.F.V.,* and *Sportsman.*

Chessie cars of the C & O with The Greenbrier, White Sulphur Springs, in the background

The New Chessie Cars on the C & O...

Beautiful new, all-stainless steel railway cars, built by Budd, are now in service on several trains of the Chesapeake and Ohio Railway.

They take you over routes rich in scenic loveliness, including the storied beauty of the Blue Ridge and Appalachian Mountains. And never have you had such opportunity to enjoy it—viewing it from the first Vista-Dome cars to go in service on any eastern railroad.

New ideas for your comfort and pleasure too numerous to catalogue, sparkle throughout these sleek and gleaming cars.

An enclosed children's nursery. Spacious private rooms. A theater. Snack bars. Music at your finger tips.

Beneath their beauty, luxury and imaginative design stands the solid fact of their all-stainless steel construction. From foundation center-sill to shining roof rail, from end-post to end-post through all their frames and girders, these cars are built of this amazing, silver-hued metal, strongest ever used in railroad car construction. Cars of stainless steel structure are built exclusively by Budd. The Budd Company, Philadelphia 32, Pennsylvania.

Budd

Carbuilder Budd Company often promoted its products through ads depicting new trains it had manufactured. In this rare magazine ad for a train would never operate in revenue service, Chesapeake & Ohio's proposed *Chessie* streamliner cruises through a countryscape painting by noted railroad-theme artist Leslie Ragan. In the background stands a lavish resort hotel, undoubtedly meant to represent the famous Greenbrier complex served by C&O at White Sulphur Springs, West Virginia. JOE WELSH COLLECTION

Largely a nocturnal operation, Nickel Plate's Chicago–Cleveland–Buffalo streamliner *Nickel Plate Limited* was rarely—if ever—photographed in color when it was new in 1950. Such was the inspiration for this oil painting by this book's editor and designer, who depicted the train shortly prior to its departure from Chicago's La Salle Street Station just after a brief bout of "lake effect" snow from nearby Lake Michigan. New Alco PA-type passenger diesels power the Pullman-Standard streamliner. ILLUSTRATION BY MIKE SCHAFER

C&O's one-time suitor, the New York, Chicago & St. Louis Railroad—the Nickel Plate—took a more modest approach to streamlining after World War II, ordering 25 new, lightweight, streamlined coaches, sleepers, and sleeper-buffet-lounge cars from Pullman-Standard. The new rolling stock was delivered in 1950 along with new PA-type passenger diesels from Alco. All went to work on the *Nickel Plate Limited*, *Westerner*, and *New Yorker* between Chicago and Buffalo, New York; selected cars operated through to metropolitan New York (Hoboken, New Jersey) on partner railroad Delaware, Lackawanna & Western east of Buffalo.

These cars were actually part of an order that had been placed by C&O (despite *The Chessie* debacle) and were therefore of similar design, except for painting and lettering. The coaches were unusual in that the main seating area was divided by center bulkheads in an effort to reduce the tunnel effect of passenger-car interiors. Car exteriors were clad in stainless-steel fluting below the windows and in dark blue paint above, with silver lettering. Nickel Plate's streamliners were attractive and entirely functional, designed more to link the railroad's modest on-line communities than to compete with parallel New York Central for Chicago–Cleveland–New York service.

C&O had a rival for Tidewater–Cincinnati service in the Norfolk & Western. Though N&W had only one "official" streamliner of its own, the all-coach *Powhatan Arrow* on a day schedule between Norfolk, Virginia, and Cincinnati, it was a classy operation. Its first new streamlined, lightweight cars arrived in 1941, but the train was not officially launched as a "new" streamliner until 1946 using the 1941 cars and some rebuilt heavyweight equipment. In 1949, the *Arrow* was completely re-equipped and its older cars shifted to its overnight companion train, the *Pocahontas*. The sides of the new Pullman-Standard streamliner were painted solid Tuscan red trimmed in gold pinstriping and lettering; the roof was black. Lounge and dining-car interiors reflected a growing postwar movement that spoke of sophistication. Inspired by the eastern Virginia legend and lore of Pocahontas, the train's Indian motif was more or less limited to its name and advertising art.

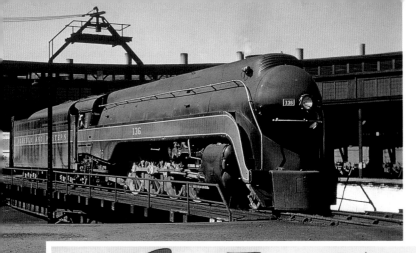

For its premier passenger services such as the *Arrow*, N&W relied on two types of handsome streamlined steam locomotives, almost to the end of the 1950s. Black with a Tuscan red flow stripe, these streamstyled steamers added a dimension of dynamics and excitement to the *Powhatan Arrow*, and the train itself brought a bit of hope and prosperity to an impoverished region of the Appalachians.

LEFT: Handsome stream-lined steam engines powered the *Powhatan Arrow*. JOHN DZIOBKO

BELOW: The *Powhatan Arrow*'s promotional folder from 1949 focused on the train's modern car interiors. MIKE SCHAFER COLLECTION

Fine New Feathers . . .

Soft lighting, modernistic bar, deep-cushioned wall divans—comfort is the purpose of the *new* Powhatan Arrow

PRESENTING the Norfolk and Western's *new* Powhatan Arrow . . . Flashing over the rails between Cincinnati and Norfolk, Va., the colorful new Arrow sets a new standard in fast, luxurious travel—new comfort, new beauty and sincere hospitality. Every new feature of this modern train is designed for one purpose —to make your trip one of genuine enjoyment. The *new* Powhatan Arrow is one of the truly fine trains of America. New coaches, new diners, new tavern-lounge-observation cars— all furnished for *everybody's* pleasure, and all designed for the ultimate in travel comfort and convenience.

New diners provide a luxurious setting for fine food and faultless service on the *new* Arrow

for the NEW Powhatan Arrow

Wide panorama windows in restful new coaches open vistas of beauty to the passenger on the *new* Arrow

Solid travel comfort is yours in the modern, roomy coaches of the new Arrow. Deep, soft, reclining seats with adjustable footrests, individual lighting, immaculate rest rooms—all designed for your comfort and convenience. Cars are equipped with automatic electric door openers, and will be serviced by a system for public address, station announcements and recorded musical programs. *You'll find a new experience in modern travel . . . on the new Powhatan Arrow*

Relaxation is a pleasure in the tastefully decorated new Tavern - Lounge - Observation Car of the *new* Arrow

The Seaboard Air Line Railroad, the first to run streamliners to Florida, heavily promoted with flashy folders. JOE WELSH COLLECTION

SUNBELT STREAMLINING

④

SUN, SAND, AND STREAMLINERS

Encouraged by the excitement generated by new trains in the Midwest and Gulf Mobile & Northern's early *Rebel* streamliners in the Deep South, Southern railroads could see the value of sticking their collective toes into the streamliner pond as the 1930s drew to a close. And nowhere would the execution be more breathtaking, both inside and out, than in the trains that served the warm, sunny region between the Carolinas and Texas—especially Florida. The trip southward started when prospective passengers made a trip to their nearest travel agent or railway ticket office and gathered a handful of promotional material such as the Seaboard Railroad's lavish folder at left. From these brochures, they could make their streamliner selection. Once they stepped aboard the *Silver Meteor*, the *Southerner*, or the *Panama Limited*, passengers were seemingly *at* their destinations, for train interiors were designed to give Northerners a taste of what it was like where they were headed. As a group, the sunbelt trains of the era exhibited a *joie de vivre* unlike their counterparts in any other region.

Florida's first streamliner was the *Silver Meteor*, launched by the Seaboard Railroad in 1939. The postwar edition of the *Meteor* is shown southbound at Washington Union Station in 1968. Today's version of the *Silver Meteor*, operated by Amtrak, has still newer cars. BOB JOHNSTON

BLAZING THE TRAIL TO FLORIDA FROM NEW YORK

Florida's seductive breezes had been attracting tourists to the Sunshine State since the late 1800s, when land development pioneer Henry M. Flagler became enamored with the area after vacationing in St. Augustine one winter. Railroads threaded their way into the state, and soon people were flocking to Florida on the Florida East Coast Railway, the Atlantic Coast Line, and the oddly name Seaboard Air Line Railroad to escape northern chills. They rode in luxurious standard trains like the *Havana Special*, the *Florida Special*, and—that flyer of

song and lore—the *Orange Blossom Special*. But not until 1939 could one ride a streamliner to Florida.

On February 2, 1939, the Seaboard Air Line debuted its lightweight *Silver Meteor*, a seven-car all-coach train operating on a fast overnight schedule between New York and Miami. Up front was one of Seaboard's slant-nosed Electro-Motive E4 diesels finished in a bright citrus scheme of yellow, orange, dark green, and silver—another celebrated livery developed by Electro-Motive. This flamboyant exterior pattern, typical of the riot of colors used in early streamliners, was picked up inside on the front of the tavern-lounge car's bar, where red leather seats with tan piping and robin's egg blue oval tables rested on a carpet of opal green and brown. In the coach section of the same car, rose-colored walls supported an orchid ceiling and brown pencil-striped upholstery alternating with patterned chamois on the seats. By contrast, the diner was done in more muted tones. An end-of-train coach observation car featured glass partitions bearing the likeness of game fish, separating the coach seating area from the lounge.

The first *Silver Meteor* was an immediate success, tapping into a seemingly limitless market for affordable luxury coach travel. In late 1939, the train was expanded to operate daily to Miami and every third day to St. Petersburg. After World War II, the popular *Silver Meteor* was re-equipped again—twice in the space of seven years. For the first time it carried streamlined sleeping and full-lounge cars, including the unique and attractive "Sun Lounge," introduced in 1956, offering a bright sun room area with oversized windows and glass in the roof (clearances north of Virginia to New York City nixed the dome-car concept that had caught on elsewhere). Driftwood lamps, seaside photomurals, and a seashell-patterned carpet in the car highlighted a beach theme. The Sun Lounge became the hallmark car of the *Meteor* well into the Amtrak era.

Not to be outdone by its rival, the Atlantic Coast Line teamed up with the Florida East Coast Railway (which carried ACL trains between Jacksonville and Miami) to introduce the *Champion* in December 1939. Providing daily service between New York and Miami, the seven-car air-conditioned trainsets were strikingly similar to the *Silver Meteor*—both were built by Budd with locomotives by Electro-Motive—but with a few twists: the train's four reclining-seat coaches featured chairs that swiveled in pairs, and one of them also contained a room for the train's hostess/maid, who took care of the children onboard and tended to other passenger needs. The train's round-end tavern-observation car featured a full bar with a marine motif backed by an etched-glass mirror.

In the late 1930s, artists from General Motors' Styling Section devised Seaboard's celebrated "citrus" locomotive paint scheme of dark green, yellow, and orange when the railroad ordered its first group of passenger diesels from GM's Electro-Motive Corporation. Some of the locomotives from this group were assigned to the famed though non-streamlined *Orange Blossom Special.* Others were assigned to the *Silver Meteor*—and so lettered—as is the case with E4 No. 3002 at Washington, D.C., circa 1940. HOWARD ROBBINS COLLECTION

Route of the *Silver Fleet*

POWERED BY GENERAL MOTORS DIESEL LOCOMOTIVES

LEFT: One of the most visually impressive pieces of advertising art from the postwar streamliner period was this scene from a series done by artist Bern Hill for Electro-Motive. The stylized scene shows a Seaboard passenger train, powered by a pair of Electro-Motive diesels, gliding through idealistic Florida scenery, rich with orange groves. BILL HOWES, VIA JOE WELSH

RIGHT: Introduced in 1956, the *Meteor's* Sun Lounge sleepers became the train's favored feature car. The glass-roofed cars (three were built by Pullman-Standard) were Seaboard's answer to the then-growing dome-car craze. Unfortunately, tight clearances in the tunnels north of the Potomac River precluded the use of dome cars on the *Meteor*, so Seaboard and Pullman-Standard instead devised the glass-roofed sleeper-lounge. This interior scene shows the car *Sun View* as it appeared in 1970. JIM NEUBAUER

FAR RIGHT: Though perhaps a bit campy by today's standards, the driftwood table lamps in the *Meteor's* Sun Lounge enhanced the car's oceanside theming. JIM NEUBAUER

Most striking were the new *Champions'* exterior colors. Two equipment sets owned by the Coast Line were fashioned with royal purple letterboards. Up front was an Electro-Motive E3 diesel also finished in royal purple and silver with gold trim, while red-and-orange Florida East Coast E3 diesels pulled the *Champion* over that carrier. Both diesel paint schemes—again, designed by Electro-Motive—were widely acknowledged as two of the most attractive in the nation, symbolizing the streamliner's break with the dingy past.

Both the *Silver Meteor* and the *Champions* were instant winners. They spawned an entire generation of other streamlined Florida trains, including an all-Pull-

ABOVE: In answer to Seaboard's *Silver Meteor*, the Atlantic Coast Line Railroad and affiliate Florida East Coast launched their own New York–Miami streamliner, the *Champion*, also in 1939. Like the *Meteor*, the "*Champ*" was wildly successful, prompting ACL and FEC to purchase additional rolling stock and add more *Champions* to serve both coasts of Florida. In this 1951 scene north of St. Augustine, the *East Coast Champion*, with at least 16 cars, hurtles along behind a pair of Electro-Motive passenger diesels sporting FEC's eye-catching red-and-yellow color scheme. H. WOLFE, SETH BRAMSON COLLECTION VIA JONATHAN NELSON

FACING PAGE: Atlantic Coast Line's early passenger diesels—one of which appears to be sweeping along with the original *Champion* of 1939—wore a flashy livery of purple and silver with yellow-gold separation stripes. (This is a famous ACL publicity scene, and the train is probably actually standing still; note its conductor poised on the ground near the very end of the train.) The cars of the first *Champion* also carried a purple letterboard. Streamliners and vibrant colors went hand in hand. H. WOLFE, SETH BRAMSON COLLECTION VIA JONATHAN NELSON

FACING PAGE, INSET: The only known color photo of the interior of the first *Champion*'s tavern-observation car reveals a décor of tropical pastels accented by chairs upholstered in wine red and brown. POWERS REPRODUCTION COMPANY VIA CSX, JOE WELSH COLLECTION

man *Florida Special* in 1949. The bright colors eventually disappeared and the two railroads merged, but the excitement begun by the *Silver Meteor* and *Champion* lasted through 1971 and the advent of Amtrak, which today operates three well-patronized *Silver* trains between New York City and several Florida destinations.

THREE WAYS FROM THE MIDWEST

When the Florida East Coast and Atlantic Coast Line launched the *Champion* in 1939, the FEC debuted a similar coach streamliner to operate a daily Miami–Jacksonville round-trip as the *Henry M. Flagler*, named after the railroad's founder. But the new lightweight arrival proved to be the catalyst for a pooled long-distance effort to Chicago between nine railroads offering three different all-coach trains every third day on three different

routes. Effectively, the arrangement offered daily service on a one-night-out schedule. Beginning in December 1940, the FEC-sponsored *Dixie Flagler*, the Pennsylvania Railroad's *South Wind*, and the Illinois Central's *City of Miami* offered three varied exterior and interior approaches to the new service. Built by Budd using its patented shot-welded fabrication process for stainless steel, the first two trains offered streamlined steam loco-motives pulling a dorm-coach-baggage car, four full

coaches, a dining car, and a round-end lounge observa-tion car. The *Flagler* was pure stainless steel, and the *South Wind* was stainless steel painted in Pennsylvania's Tuscan red. Murals of Florida scenes adorned bulkheads in the coaches; the trains featured on-board stewardess-nurse service and an Art Deco-styled train radio in the lounge car.

The IC's *City of Miami* offered not only those ameni-ties, but far more. Electro-Motive and Pullman-Standard

designers came up with a splashy orange train accented with a green wave pattern bracketed by crimson striping that swooped up from the slant-nosed locomotive's front wheels and "splashed" down to track level. A similar band ran along the tops of the cars and cut a swath downward to form an arrow on rear observation car *Bamboo Grove*. One of the four coaches was set aside as a "women and children's coach," a common practice during the World War II era. Each car interior utilized different mixes of

yellow, copper, tan, blue, green, and coral to make them different from each other. All boasted the use of native woods for decorative trim. In the observation car, coral leather accented the booths; tables were made of zebra wood with a Formica coating. A natural bamboo bar with a canopy fronted a mural of a Florida beach scene juxtaposed with a map of the train's route and principle stations, which were lighted along the way to indicate the next stop. Alas, this supernova of streamliner art lasted

STYLING A STREAMLINER'S CLOAKING

It's 1946 and the war is over. You're trying to get your railroad into the modern era with freight diesels and passenger streamliners. The salesman from Electro-Motive has his order book out. He can get you a spot on the production line six months from now for a dozen freight and four passenger locomotives for your new streamliner. How do you want them painted?

Painted, you say? For the last century, your steam engines have been black with a graphite smokebox, red cab roof, and white numerals on the tender. Your heavyweight, battleship passenger cars built in the 1920s have always been Pullman green with gold lettering. But that's not much of a "new image." The Pennsylvania Railroad can afford to hire an industrial designer like Raymond Loewy and the New York Central a Henry Dreyfuss, but all you can scrape up is a draftsman in your railroad's mechanical department who happens to do watercolors of horses. Besides, you can't *afford* a designer and your railroad doesn't have the spare manpower to take the time to develop a new corporate image from scratch.

But in six months there will be 70 feet of butterscotch-colored primer on the flank of your new E7. The Electro-Motive salesman repeats the question, "How do you want it painted?"

This was not an unusual situation in the 1940s, and the Electro-Motive Division of General Motors had a handy answer. Since 1937 GM had been designing paint schemes for its customers, and the EMD Styling Section at the locomotive factory in LaGrange, Illinois, near Chicago, had a staff of artists to create appropriate and colorful liveries for railroads that never really had dealt with the problem before.

At a typical sales meeting, the EMD rep would show the railroad's mechanical, public relations, and advertising people sample renderings of various paint schemes. The company's colors and traditions would be considered, but often the concept was created "from scratch" as combinations or variations of the sample liveries. The railroad's input was turned over to the Styling Section, and an EMD artist would work up some rough sketches

A scene from the Styling Section of General Motors' locomotive-building subsidiary Electro-Motive Division shows (left to right) Ben Dedek, Bob Flodine, Ed Moreau, and Lee Buchholz reviewing paint-scheme proposals circa 1950. Various railroads are represented, including Pennsylvania, the Alaska Railroad, and Denver & Rio Grande Western. Of particular note is the Ben Dedek rendering in the foreground of Illinois Central E8-series locomotives wearing brown and orange. EMD

of the proposed ideas. The customer would approve or modify them, and then the artists would return to the drawing board to render a final proposal in full color artwork. Once approved, the final version would be converted into blueprints for the paint shop, and the locomotive would receive the new image.

This happened so often that the EMD artists created or influenced almost every railroad paint scheme developed between 1937 and 1960. It was their sense of Art Deco style that resulted in the uniformly high quality of the "streamline era" paint schemes throughout the industry. The EMD stylists paid attention to detail and had a sense of tasteful style and color usage that gave the entire postwar era its distinctive "look."

The Styling Section had its origins in the General Motors Detroit automobile-styling departments. One of its earliest triumphs was probably the most famous locomotive paint scheme of all times, the Santa Fe "warbonnet." In 1937 the railroad was ordering the first new "streamliner" E1A passenger units for the newly streamlined *Super Chief*. The railroad's designer, Sterling

McDonald, had developed a Southwest American Indian theme for the train, and architects Paul Cret and John Harbeson were working with the Budd company to create the interiors for the passenger cars. The task of styling the locomotive was assigned to Leland Knickerbocker of GM's Art & Color Industrial Design Department, who picked up McDonald's Indian motif. He began with a brilliant red "face" and swept it back along the stainless-steel side in a pattern reminiscent of the traditional feathered war-bonnet. He modified the round Santa Fe herald into a large yellow oval, which he spread across the nose. The end result was absolutely stunning—and long-lived (chapter five). It was being applied to new Santa Fe freight locomotives well into the 1990s!

Leland Knickerbocker and Paul Meyer handled most of the GM prewar styling and set the tone for everything that would follow. Among their best-known images were the Southern Railway's green and gold (based on the railroad's established steam locomotive colors), the Rock Island's red, silver, and maroon *Rockets*, and, from Meyer, Illinois Central's classic orange-and-chocolate *Panama Limited* livery of 1942. In 1939 they worked closely with designer Raymond Loewy on the Missouri Pacific's new *Eagle*.

Leland Knickerbocker died in 1940 at the age of 46, just as EMD was establishing its new locomotive factory in LaGrange. A year later the new Styling Section was set up at LaGrange under John Markestein, who had both engineering and artwork experience. Markestein gathered an impressive array of skilled artists including Ben Dedek and Harry Bockewicz, whose names showed up on much of the finished artwork. They continued the same dedication to style and detail that Knickerbocker and Meyer had pioneered in Detroit. Because so many railroads were anxious to dieselize as rapidly as possible, the companies made extensive use of the Styling Section, and, as a result, nearly every "first generation" diesel livery displayed the same sense of Art Deco style. The EMD designers used uniform styling "elements" like edge stripes and nose

curves that flowed with the natural lines of the locomotive and usually lined up on the rivet strips on the carbody sides. They never "fought" the natural contours of the locomotive, as is often the case with contemporary car and diesel schemes. Quite often, the scheme developed by EMD was adapted to the passenger rolling stock as well.

The railroads that never bought EMD or availed themselves of the services of the Styling Section usually had paint schemes that were distinctly "different," though certainly not unattractive. The New Haven and Nickel Plate are excellent examples of railroads that had non-EMD schemes. The styling of second-generation locomotives following the 1960s was usually done by non-railroad artists and designers whose work today often looks chaotic and garish compared to the uniformly tasteful Art Deco styling of the 1940s and 1950s.

By the good fortune of time and place, the small group of artists in Detroit and LaGrange established an era of quality that will be the benchmark of railroad styling for all time. They gave the "Streamline Era" its defining essence.—*Jim Boyd*

A color scheme that never was. This Electro-Motive proposal for Illinois Central was likely intended for the company's new *Panama Limited* streamliner of 1942. Using the colors introduced on IC's 1940 *City of Miami* (pages 70–71) but employing increasingly sophisticated lines and patterns, artist Ben Dedek created this spectacular scheme that included silver pinstriping. In the end, a less-flamboyant but still eye-catching livery prevailed. Orange was swapped for green in the "swoop" stripe, yellow for silver in the pinstriping, and brown for orange; overall design patterns remained the same. The result was an IC classic (following page) that would endure, albeit with minor modifications, for nearly 30 years. EMD

Illinois Central's premier streamliner was the Chicago–New Orleans *Panama Limited*, shown northbound in 1969 crossing Pass Manchack, 40 miles north of New Orleans. From 1942 to the early 1970s, IC passenger trains wore the striking color combination of brown and orange with yellow stripes, developed by Electro-Motive. Compare this with the proposed IC scheme appearing on the previous page. JIM BOYD.

only until just after World War II, when the IC decided to repaint the train in the chocolate-and-orange scheme established by the line's most recent streamlining endeavor, the *Panama Limited*. But as a complete package, the *City of Miami* still remains a yardstick against which any lightweight speedster must be judged.

GEMS TO NEW ORLEANS AND THE DEEP SOUTH

Illinois Central's all-sleeping-car *Panama Limited* made the leap to streamlined status in 1942 just as America was becoming fully immersed in World War II. Though the train's lightweight sleepers were by this time standard issue—the same configurations were popping up around

the country as railroads refurbished their trains—the *Panama*'s feature cars reflected the same flair Pullman-Standard designers had exhibited with IC's *City of Miami*. The diners had several interior partitions festooned with photomurals of the Deep South. Cocktail table alcoves at each end of the dining room offered full-length draperies that could be drawn around the table for a secluded effect. Other cozy lounges were located in half of a mid-train sleeper, which sported wrought iron-accented doors and furniture to evoke a French Quarter theme. In the round-end sleeper observation car, bamboo-framed furniture, squared etched glass on exterior windows, and flowered curtains between them continued the French Quarter influence. On the observation car's outside flanks, a yel-

Beauty aboard the "City of New Orleans" is more than skin deep. It includes colors soft and restful to the eye after a full day's travel . . . seats beautifully molded to support the body and adjustable at the touch of a button. . . . leg rests that actually support the entire leg . . . Venetian blinds as easy to operate as they are handsome.

low neon sign glowed proudly with the train's name. Additional new sleepers came on line early in the 1950s, and the train's service remained impeccable nearly to the end in 1971. In the 1960s, a five-course gourmet "King's Dinner," complete with cocktails and wine for about $10, provided a fitting grand finale to the *Panama Limited*'s legacy. Late in 1967, IC introduced a "new" Chicago–New Orleans coach streamliner, the *Magnolia Star*. Chicago media personnel who turned out for the train's inaugural were miffed to discover that it was merely coaches and a cafe-club car added to the *Panama Limited*.

A daylight, all-coach *City of New Orleans* made its debut on the same route in 1947 incorporating many of the style elements of the *Panama*'s lounges and diners,

with Deep South scenes on coach bulkheads and luxurious parlor-car seating on the train's 8 A.M.-to-midnight, 900-plus mile run. The Illinois Central knew its *City* clientele would spend more waking hours enjoying the train's amenities than patrons on the overnight run, so it provided a stewardess, full dining car, and tavern-lounge observation where no detail was spared—both artistically and in personal service. Because large numbers of passengers traveled to rural destinations, however, the train's exclusive trappings were not well-patronized and were discontinued. Ridership remained strong, though, and the *City of New Orleans* train name eventually became the standard bearer on an overnight run under Amtrak after the *City* had been immortalized in a popular song.

Daytime running mate to IC's *Panama Limited* was the legendary *City of New Orleans*. The brochure issued for the new coach streamliner was full of idyllic scenes of travelers (with men almost always wearing suits, no less) enjoying the day-long journey between Chicago and New Orleans. This coach scene shows bulkhead murals with a French Quarter touch. MIKE SCHAFER COLLECTION

THE SOUTHERNER

Streamliner
NEW YORK . . . NEW ORLEANS
via ATLANTA and BIRMINGHAM

SOUTHERN

The Southerner

THE SOUTHERN SR SERVES THE SOUTH

SOUTHERN RAILWAY SYSTEM

Two more Deep South streamliners were inaugurated in 1941, when the then-conservative Southern Railroad launched the New York–New Orleans *Southerner* and the Washington–Memphis *Tennessean*. Both trains carried streamlined coaches, diners, and tavern-lounge observation cars. The lightweight cars were constructed of cheaper Cor-Ten steel alloy but cosmetically finished in more expensive stainless-steel sheathing—no doubt to resemble Budd's all-stainless trains (at the time, only the Budd Company held the patent necessary to fabricate all-stainless-steel carbodies). Utilizing predominantly blues and greens, the interiors of the modern trains featured air-conditioning, bright colors, indirect lighting, and plenty of space for passengers to stretch out—a radical departure from what the coach passenger had suffered through in the pre-streamlined era. The tavern-lounges sported a chrome-trimmed stand-up bar, etched glass dividers, and modern cocktail tables and chairs. Coach seats reclined and swiveled, and oversized

LUNCHEON

The SOUTHERNER

washroom facilities were available for both men and women—a welcome change from the heavyweight era. Famous southern cooking was available in the dining car.

From Washington south, the *Southerner* was hauled by a modern slant-nosed Electro-Motive E6 diesel attired in Southern's classy Virginia green, gold, and aluminum finish. Between Washington and Bristol, the *Tennessean* was pulled by bullet-nosed streamlined steam locomotives of the Southern (styled by Otto Kuhler) and Norfolk & Western. Southern E6 diesels took over from Bristol to Memphis.

Inspired by the success of the prewar *Southerner* and the *Tennessean*, Southern decided to streamline its venerable *Crescent* after World War II. As a premier New York–New Orleans entry, the *Crescent* received new lightweight sleeping cars, sleeper-lounges, diners, and coaches by 1950. One outstanding feature was the raised "Lookout Lounge" sleeper-observation car. Here, passengers in elevated rear- and side-facing seats enjoyed the view through oversized windows. Another innovation was the master room, the roomiest sleeping accommodation on rails, sleeping three and boasting a private shower. In the postwar period, master rooms could be found on only one other train: Pennsy's all-Pullman *Broadway Limited*.

Southern ran its *Southern Crescent* (a direct descendent using the route of the *Southerner* and many of the

RIGHT: For the 1940 debut of the *Southern Belle*, Margaret Landry of Baton Rouge, Louisiana, was chosen among several contestants to personify the new streamliner. She appeared, suitably costumed, in numerous publicity photos such as this, as well as on KCS public passenger timetables, helping to make the *Southern Belle* the "Sweetheart of American Trains." KCS, GERALD HOOK COLLECTION

BELOW: Originally, the *Southern Belle* wore a dark, Brunswick green, exaggerated a mite in this linen postcard from circa 1940. The green later was changed to black. MIKE SCHAFER COLLECTION

THE *Southern Belle*
"SWEETHEART OF AMERICAN TRAINS"

features of the *Crescent*) until 1979, when the railroad finally joined the national carrier Amtrak—ending the last great example of a privately operated overnight streamliner in the U.S.

Other trains that served New Orleans also capitalized on that city's unique charm as inspiration. Offering service over a Kansas City Southern route that once was deemed too slow for a fast passenger train, the post–World War II *Southern Belle* instilled speed and a touch of class between Kansas City and its dual southern termini of New Orleans and Port Arthur, Texas. The train split in two at Shreveport, Louisiana, from which station its tavern-lounge observation went to New Orleans with a sleeper, coaches, and the diner, while another diner was added for the Port Arthur section. Oversize-window coaches added as late as 1965, brightly colored interiors throughout, and a stunning equipment design scheme of black cars trimmed with red and yellow lines gave this postwar streamliner a magnificent presence wherever it roamed.

Another train serving New Orleans was Louisville & Nashville's Navy blue *Humming Bird*. Departing every night from Cincinnati's awe-inspiring Art Deco Union Terminal and in the morning from the Crescent City, passengers were treated to a daylight run over the bayous and inlets along the Gulf Coast between New Orleans and Mobile. And a perfect place to view the unique scenery was the glass-partitioned full-length club-lounge car, complete with a palm tree mural and oversize windows. Similarly appointed dining cars featured country-ham breakfasts, Gulf Coast seafood platters, shrimp Creole, "and other Southern Dishes famous on L&N diners."

STAR OF THE LONE STAR STATE

Finally, one of the most colorful north-south sunbelt trains of the postwar period was the *Texas Special*, introduced in May 1948. Jointly operated by the St. Louis-San Francisco Railway (the "Frisco") and the Missouri-Kansas-Texas Railroad (the "Katy"), the train linked St. Louis with San Antonio via Dallas, with sections serving Fort Worth and Wichita Falls, Texas. The *Special*'s flashy stainless-steel-sheathed cars built by Pullman-Standard were trimmed with red roofs, window panels, and skirting. Its Electro-Motive locomotives were some of the very few that carried decorative stainless-steel trim to blend in with the train. On their nose, along with the train's name in stylized script, was a lone star—for Texas. The new train offered modern reclining-seat coaches and a coach-buffet-lounge where passengers could enjoy refreshments or, while praying for smooth track, drop a line to relatives at a writing desk. The *Special*'s new lightweight sleeping cars offered roomettes (for one) and bedrooms (for two).

MEET THE *New* TEXAS SPECIAL

M·K·T
KATY RAILROAD
MISSOURI-KANSAS-TEXAS

FRISCO

Streamliners

First-class passengers were afforded a fine view of Texas sagebrush country from the rearward-facing seats of the the sleeper-lounge observation car. All of the *Special's* cars were named either for geographic locations along the line or for famous Missourians or Texan heroes such as Davy Crockett and Sam Houston.

Due to its early success, the railroad had to press rebuilt heavyweight cars (some painted with fake "shadowlining" to simulate stainless steel) into the train's otherwise streamlined consist to accommodate demand. But the *Special* fell from grace in the late 1950s as riders abandoned streamliners for the auto and airliner, and parent Katy focused its attention on where the money really was: freight traffic. Disgusted with poor timekeeping on the Katy segment of the run, the Frisco pulled out of the joint operation in 1959. The train was shifted to an all-Katy routing by changing the northern terminus to Kansas City. Now down to mostly mail and express cars and a couple of coaches, the skeletal remnants of the once-great train soldiered on until 1965, when it was discontinued.

ABOVE: The brochure cover for the joint Katy–Frisco *Texas Special* was as colorful as the train itself. JOE WELSH COLLECTION

BELOW: With its stainless-steel exterior accented in bright red, the *Texas Special* was one of the most vibrant postwar streamliners, yet it was rarely photographed in color. The northbound *Special* at Waco, Texas, in 1954 shows off the still-bright look of the six-year-old train. S. C. GREGORY, COLLECTION OF ROBERT P. SCHMIDT

Considered by rail historians to be the finest paint scheme ever to grace a locomotive, Santa Fe's "Warbonnet" livery adorns early Electro-Motive diesels. JIM BOYD

WESTERN DREAMLINING

5

STREAMLINING THE TRANSCONS OF THE AMERICAN WEST

The lure of the American West had drawn rail travelers for nearly 70 years before the streamliner came along. The ultra-long-distance traveler was the railroads' most lucrative customer, and for years the railroads had carried them on such great heavyweight trains originating from Chicago as Santa Fe's *California Limited*, the joint North Western-Union Pacific-Southern Pacific *Overland Limited*, or the Burlington-Rio Grande-Western Pacific *Exposition Flyer*. It's not surprising that Western trains immediately received the full attention of the industrial designer. Union Pacific's early streamliners to Portland, Los Angeles, and San Francisco were the first Western transcontinental lightweights (chapter 2). Other railroads followed, and after World War II, a new battle for the cross-country traveler was joined. With spectacular scenery outside the window and attractive surroundings inside, the new trains of the West represented the best the streamliner movement had to offer.

THE SANTA FE

Super Chief

As with most new streamliners of the era, Santa Fe promoted its 1937 *Super Chief* streamliner through the printed media, issuing a large, two-color brochure whose cover contrasted the train's sleekness with a venerable steam locomotive. The artist also managed to hint at the train's interior by including Indian artwork borders. JOE WELSH COLLECTION

SANTA FE'S CHICAGO–LOS ANGELES SPEEDWAY

In response to the May 1936 introduction of Union Pacific's *City of Los Angeles* streamliner, the Atchison, Topeka & Santa Fe hastily inaugurated a heavyweight all-Pullman *Super Chief* as its flagship on the Chicago–Los Angeles route in the same month. Although faultlessly executed, the dark green standard train lacked the modern styling of UP's bright new lightweight. Determined to remain competitive, Santa Fe approached the Budd Company of Philadelphia for a single streamlined *Super Chief* of its own that would be introduced in May

1937. This once-in-a-blue-moon train would become perhaps the most attractive streamliner ever built.

Santa Fe's request brought together a talented team of designers with one goal in mind: fashion a train that reflected modern design but also highlighted Santa Fe's longstanding link with Native American art of the Southwest. Chicago designer Sterling McDonald, a contributor on Union Pacific's first trains, was hired to consult on the interior design and colors of the *Super Chief*. Inspired by a trip into Indian country and by the advice of Roger Birdseye, Santa Fe's advertising guru and an expert on Indian art, McDonald's interior perspectives were converted into full sized mock-ups. Now thoroughly warmed to the subject, Santa Fe turned McDonald's work over to Budd architects Paul Cret and John Harbeson, who would bring the project home. The results were magical.

What distinguished the new train were its interiors. Harbeson had found a product named "Flexwood" that would allow him to panel the interiors of the *Super Chief* in rare woods. His palette was limitless. The names of the exotic woods tripped off the tongue and suggested variety and beauty; bubinga, maccassar, ribbon primavera, satinwood, teak, ebony, and a dozen other woods all conspired to make the inside of the *Super Chief* exquisite. Coupled with the smartly executed Indian theme, the interiors were one of a kind.

The lounge observation car, aptly named *Navajo,* was typical. Under a ceiling of turquoise framed by copper-colored walls sat easy chairs finished in a bluish purple, red, and cream reproduction of an Indian woven blanket. The mill that produced the fabric was even instructed to drop a stitch occasionally to resemble handmade blanketry. On the walls between the windows were genuine Indian sand paintings telling the story of the "Myth of the Mountain Chant" as handed down by Navajo prophets. At the rear solarium of the car was a goatskin-shaded silver ceremonial-knife lamp.

Lounge car *Acoma* represented a confluence of Indian art and rare woods. Walls of birdseye cypress supported a ceiling of primavera wood. Navajo patterns adorned the window shades, but the centerpiece of the car was the bar in the cocktail lounge. The bar front was finished in attractive zebra wood while behind it was a spectacular inlaid wood rendering of a Kachina—an Indian ceremonial dancer.

The train's diner and sleeping cars were also finished in rare woods. Outside, the nine-car non-articulated stainless-steel train gleamed like polished silver. Up front was a new streamlined two-unit E1 diesel

in cab-and-booster configuration from the Electro-Motive Corporation attired in what many believe was the finest locomotive paint scheme ever created. Styled by General Motors' talented artist Leland Knickerbocker (see "Styling the Streamliners" in chapter 4), crimson paint gracefully flowed back from the nose and along the flanks of the silver locomotive suggesting, as the artist put it, "the profile of an Indian head and the trailing feathers of a warbonnet." Highlighted with yellow and black, the scheme would become world famous.

The *Super*'s older cousin, the all-Pullman *Chief,* was streamlined in January 1938. Its six lightweight equipment sets allowed Santa Fe to advertise daily streamlined service between Chicago and Los Angeles. Built largely by Pullman-Standard but with diners and lounge cars from Budd, the *Chief* lacked the exotic wood interiors of the first *Super Chief,* but its cars were still attractive.

Less than month after the arrival of the *Chief,* Santa Fe introduced another lightweight train on the Chicago–

In a publicity scene incorporating the new 1937 *Super Chief,* passengers and bystanders at Santa Fe's Albuquerque station fawn over the train and examine the wares being sold on the platform by local Native Americans—a long-standing tradition at the Albuquerque stop. BUDD COMPANY, HAGLEY MUSEUM AND LIBRARY, JOE WELSH COLLECTION

Passenger-train advertising was once as common in national magazines as automobile ads are today. This dreamy ad from Santa Fe appeared in the December 17, 1949, issue of the *Saturday Evening Post* and elsewhere to promote the *Chief* fleet in general. In an era when many train advertisements had an almost cartoonlike quality, this piece of artwork was a welcome—almost breathtaking—change. MIKE SCHAFER COLLECTION

The **Chiefs**

BETWEEN CHICAGO AND THE WEST AND SOUTHWEST

Santa Fe

Headed by the *Super Chief* and *The Chief*, the Santa Fe great fleet of trains between Chicago and California offers a choice of fine accommodations to satisfy every taste and fit every pocketbook. And between Chicago and Texas, it's the *Texas Chief*.

For smooth-riding comfort...friendly hospitality... delicious Fred Harvey meals...fascinating scenery...travel Santa Fe—*the Chief Way!*

R. T. Anderson, General Passenger Traffic Manager, Santa Fe System Lines, Chicago 4, Illinois

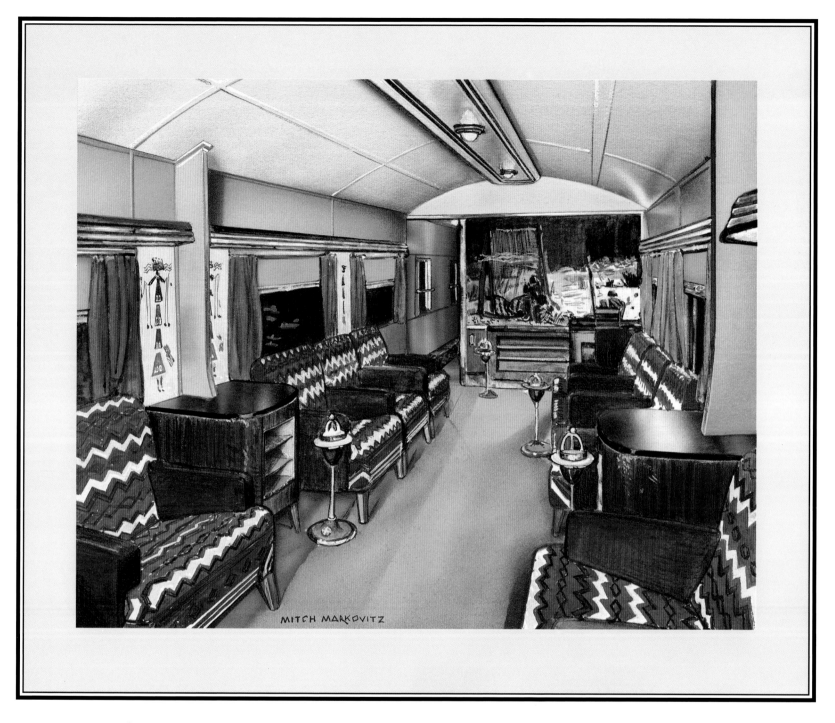

Lounge observation car *Navajo* of Santa Fe's 1937 *Super Chief*, looking forward from the observation end. On the bulkhead at the forward end of the lounge area was a sepia-tone photo screened onto canvas. It depicted Navajo women weaving their traditional blankets with the same flame-stitch design duplicated in the car's upholstery. It doesn't appear that drinks normally were served in the Navajo lounge, but that it was used mainly for socializing, smoking, and viewing. Cocktails could be had in the *Acoma*, the *Super's* dormitory-lounge car at the head end of the train.
ILLUSTRATION BY MITCH MARKOVITZ

MARY COLTER

One of the most longstanding design relationships in twentieth century railroading was the link between the Santa Fe Railway and Native American art of the Southwest. The association can largely be attributed to the influence of the Fred Harvey Company. Famous for its meals and accommodations, Harvey built an empire for itself with a series of great hotels and restaurants, mostly in the American Southwest. Many were served by the Santa Fe. The railroad also used the Harvey Company to provide its dining-car service, and a symbiotic relationship between the two companies developed.

Born in 1869, talented Mary Elizabeth Jane Colter was first contracted by the Fred Harvey Company in 1902 to decorate the Alvarado Hotel and its adjacent Indian Museum at Albuquerque, New Mexico. Later she designed or decorated other great Harvey facilities that drew on the architecture of Native Americans and the Southwest, including "Hopi House," a pueblo-style structure at the south rim of the Grand Canyon.

Harvey and Santa Fe's fascination with Native American themes greatly influenced the advertising for early Santa Fe trains, including the de Luxe and the California Limited. In 1936 Santa Fe introduced its premier Super Chief between Chicago and Los Angeles. For this new train, Mary Colter was commissioned to design a special pattern of china. Drawing on the art of the Mimbres tribe dating from 1100 A.D., she created 39 beautiful red-and-black-on-ivory pieces. This distinctive Mimbreno china, featuring animal pictographs, continued to grace the tables of the Super Chief, on which it was used exclusively, for years. Today, Mimbreno china remains highly prized and collectible.

Champagne Dinner on the *Super Chief* in 1972, served on Mimbreno china designed some 35 years earlier by Mary Colter. BOB JOHNSTON

Los Angeles run. This Budd-built five-car speedster was christened as *El Capitan* and operated on the *Super Chief*'s hot schedule, following that train by minutes. Unlike the *Super Chief* and *Chief*, the "*El Cap*" was an all-coach train that featured a lunch-counter diner, reclining-seat coaches, a coach observation car, and other amenities including a courier nurse. Then immediately on the heels of *El Capitan*'s delivery, Santa Fe received another set of *Super Chief* equipment similar to that of the *Chief* (the interior design of the original *Super Chief* streamliner would never be duplicated). The railroad suddenly had the distinction of operating the largest number of streamlined trains in the nation.

The Santa Fe fleet continued to grow both before and after World War II, with enough new cars added so as to permit daily operation of both the *Super Chief* and *El Capitan*. In the final versions of these trains, the railroad achieved the pinnacle of postwar design. The 1951 *Super*—the last edition built—featured modern room accommodations and a stylish round-end sleeper-lounge observation car. For passengers seeking a diversion on the 39-hour excursion, the *Super Chief*'s new Pleasure Dome lounge was *the* place to socialize. This unique car offered a modern lounge on the main level, swiveling parlor chairs in the upper-level dome, a cocktail lounge under the dome, and a private dining room—the Turquoise Room—for dinner parties. (The Pleasure Dome was always operated adjacent to the regular dining car so that the Turquoise Room could be served from the diner's kitchen.)

The final edition *El Capitan*, introduced in 1956, was a landmark train that would influence the next generation of American railroad passenger-car design. The entire *El Capitan* was re-equipped with double decked "Hi-Level" cars. While the advantages of bilevel car design had already been applied to commuter rail cars, *El Capitan* represented the first application of the concept to an American long-distance train. In addition to the extra passenger capacity gained by moving baggage storage and restrooms to the lower level, keeping the passengers on the upper floor eight feet above the rails improved the ride quality and the view.

DINING PENTHOUSE STYLE

The spacious dining room on the scenic Hi-Level offers a selection of tasty Fred Harvey meals priced to fit your travel budget.

MEN ONLY

...ounge-dressing rooms on the lower level ...ch chair car have large wash basins ...ther conveniences that men like, including ...ent electric plugs to keep all ...ic-shavers happy.

INDIANS AND SCENERY ALONG YOUR WAY

You travel through the colorful Indian country of New Mexico during daylight hours. From the wide windows of the Hi-Level cars you can enjoy a wonderful view of the scenery including the picturesque and age-old Indian Pueblo villages along the route of El Capitan.

Tops in fun **"TOP OF THE CAP" LOUNGE**

Designed for pleasure from end to end, from top to bottom. You can sip your favorite refreshment upstairs and enjoy magnificent vistas from this scenic Hi-Level. Or you can step down to the Coffee Shop in the Kachina Lounge on the lower level to enjoy a "snack" from early morning until midnight.

ABOVE: Newly equipped with "Hi-Level" cars, *El Capitan* of 1956 rated an excellent brochure that illustrated how the bilevel train was laid out. MIKE SCHAFER COLLECTION

BELOW: Running combined as a single train, the westbound *El Capitan/Super Chief* glides through Raton Pass, New Mexico, in September 1969. Forward in the train are *El Cap*'s Hi-Level cars. The single-level *Super Chief* section features the Pleasure Dome car, which housed the Turquoise Room. BOB JOHNSTON

INSET: Overlooking the tables of the Turquoise Room dining area on the *Super Chief* was this turquoise medallion wall art, lit by indirect lighting. JIM HEUER

The City of San Francisco
pacemaker for trains to come

Every three days a sleek golden yellow streamliner glides out of Chicago, and another out of San Francisco. In one day and two nights these famous Overland Route trains span two-thirds of the continent...over the Rockies ...skimming across Great Salt Lake on the spectacular Lucin Causeway... through Reno and over the High Sierra. These are the finest, fastest trains between Chicago and San Francisco.

If you have ridden the Streamliner *City of San Francisco*, you remember the smooth gliding speed, the spacious cars and luxurious sleeping rooms, the superb food and service. It is like a fine hotel, on wheels.

On the *City of San Francisco* (Chicago-San Francisco), the *Daylights* and the *Lark* (San Francisco-Los Angeles) and the *Sunbeams* (Houston-Dallas), Southern Pacific tested many modern ideas in years of daily service. This experience gave us a head start in designing the trains to come.

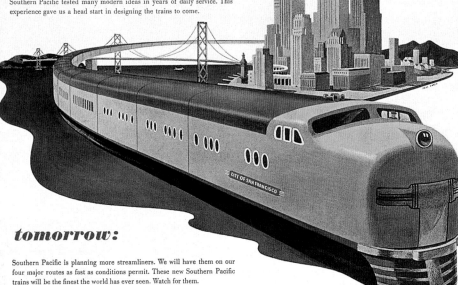

tomorrow:

Southern Pacific is planning more streamliners. We will have them on our four major routes as fast as conditions permit. These new Southern Pacific trains will be the finest the world has ever seen. Watch for them.

P.S. While Southern Pacific trains are still busy returning veterans to their homes, we believe that by summer travel conditions will be somewhere near normal again. So if you are planning a trip to California this summer, we look forward to the pleasure of having you as a guest on our trains. Be sure your ticket reads *Southern Pacific*, the West's greatest railroad—route of the *City of San Francisco*, the *Daylights*, the *Lark* and the *Sunbeams*.

S·P The friendly Southern Pacific

Four scenic routes to California. Go on one, return on another. See twice as much!

Sand drawings and metalwork adorning the cars still reflected the Native American influence. The upstairs of the train's Hi-Level lounge car featured the "Top of the Cap" club section under a curving glass ceiling; adjacent was a complete newsstand. Downstairs, snacks, sandwiches, and light refreshments were available in the Kachina Coffee Shop. Because the kitchen was down below, the dining car's upstairs area could seat 80 passengers at a time, a far cry from the normal 48 in a single-level car. Kitchen personnel also had much more room.

This new *El Capitan* proved so popular and yet so practical from an operating standpoint that Santa Fe continued to acquire additional Hi-Level coaches into the 1960s for other trains. Convinced of the bilevel design's merits, Amtrak would choose the concept for its own new fleet of long-distance cars—dubbed "Superliners." Today, new Superliners and former Santa Fe Hi-Level cars can be seen on long-distance trains across the nation.

IN SERVICE
THURSDAY JULY 8TH
BETWEEN
CHICAGO···
SAN FRANCISCO

ABOVE: In this oversize magazine ad from Southern Pacific, a stylized version of the 1939 *City of San Francisco* swoops in over the Golden Gate Bridge and the train's namesake metropolis. Judging by the ad copy, this classic advertisement ran in the spring of 1946. MIKE MC BRIDE COLLECTION

RIGHT: The *Forty-Niner* was a steam-powered streamliner introduced in 1937 between Chicago and Oakland/San Francisco as a supplement to the *City of San Francisco*. The train relied largely on rebuilt heavyweight equipment and colorful, shrouded steam locomotives. JOE WELSH COLLECTION

THE FORTY NINER

THE OVERLAND ROUTE

UNION PACIFIC TO THE WEST COAST

Not content to rest on the laurels earned from the 1936 launching of the *City of Los Angeles* and *City of San Francisco*, the Union Pacific continued to upgrade its Western streamliner fleet. In late 1937 it took delivery from Pullman-Standard of two new 14-car sets of equipment for the *City of Los Angeles* and *City of San Francisco*. By now the cars had evolved into full-sized vehicles, but UP still clung to the concept of articulation, and some of the cars in the train were built as two-unit sets.

Without question, the most spectacular car design on either 1937 train was the *City of Los Angeles'* lounge car, *Little Nugget*. In contrast to the ultra-modern interiors of the rest of the train, the *Little Nugget* replicated a Wild West saloon of the late 1800s complete with fake gas lights and an electrically animated singing canary in a gilt cage over the bar. (An apocryphal story attributes the eventual demise of the probably annoying canary to a direct hit from a well-aimed seltzer bottle.)

The 1937 train was pulled by a threesome of Electro-Motive E2 diesels clad in leaf brown and Armour yellow. Two other *City of Los Angeles* and *City of San Francisco* equipment sets soon followed in 1941. These two trains were finished in what would become the new standard Union Pacific passenger train scheme: Armour yellow and gray with red lettering and striping. While the rest of the trains' interiors reflected the basic designs of the time, once again it was a *City of Los Angeles* lounge car that stole the show. Unlike the *Little Nugget* operating on one of the other *City of L.A.* equipment sets, the *Hollywood* lounge car featured the latest in materials. Furniture and wall panels were constructed of a radical new material known as Formica. Lucite and Nylon also debuted. The car's round windows were made of Polaroid glass that could be rotated with a hand crank to screen out glare.

After World War II, the *City of Los Angeles* continued to operate as one of Union Pacific's top trains. Consistently strong patronage and the fine trains offered by competing carriers convinced the Union Pacific to invest in additional equipment, including dome cars. Dome coaches, dome-lounge observation cars, and dome diners arrived in 1955. These "Astra Domes"—as UP called

ABOVE: Swank social center of the 1941 *City of Los Angeles* was lounge car *Hollywood*, which—like the homebuilt lounge car *Copper King* appearing on the 1938 *City of Los Angeles*—featured portholed Polaroid windows (note the cranks for rotating the glass to reduce glare). Interior decor featured a white window band with line art between the portholes and futuristic metallic silver banding on the upper side walls. UNION PACIFIC MUSEUM COLLECTION, IMAGE NO. 1614-B-18

BELOW: The dome-lounge observation cars delivered for *City of Los Angeles* and other *City* services in 1955 featured an under-dome bar area paneled in wormwood. Behind the bar was a mural of a Union Pacific turbine locomotive and (not visible in this 1971 view) the M-10000 streamliner. MIKE SCHAFER

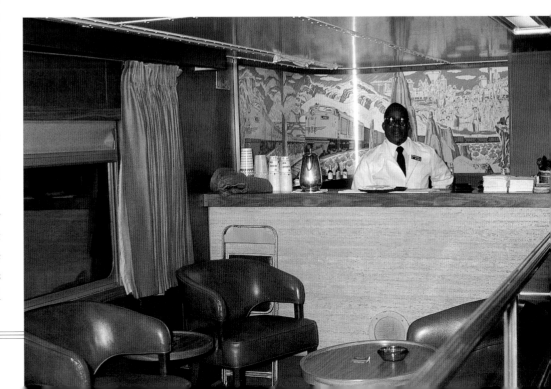

them—would be assigned to the *City of Los Angeles* as well as the *City of Portland, Los Angeles Challenger, City of St. Louis,* and *City of Denver.* No other railroad in America featured dome dining, and the unique cars presented the most elegant dining experience on rails. Under a glass dome, passengers could dine by starlight or watch the passing scenery while feasting on cuisine that rose miles above typical railroad fare. On the lower level, the car's main dining room featured restaurant-style round tables, a rarity on railroad diners. Below the dome was a reserved dining area for

groups. Although the dome diners were withdrawn from service in 1970, the remainder of this final memorable version of the *City of Los Angeles* lasted into 1971, a direct descendent of a diminutive three-car train—the M-10000—that had helped make "streamliner" a household word.

A GOLDEN OPPORTUNITY LOST

As joint players in the hotly competitive Chicago–Los Angeles travel market, Southern Pacific and the Chicago, Rock Island & Pacific were the underdog team. Their first (and only) transcontinental-

THE
Astra Dome
DINING CAR

Union Pacific introduces the **first** dome-type dining car for travelers between Chicago and the Pacific Coast.

Here's a new and delightful experience in travel; "roof garden" dining in a picture window setting. While enjoying your selection of superb, freshly prepared foods, you can feast your eyes on magnificent panoramic views stretching to the far horizon. You'll find it to be a bright page in your book of memories.

The Gold Room, with gold plated dinner service, available for small private parties.

There's a glow of glamour in both the intimate private Gold Room and the larger, or main dining room on the lower floor of the Astra Dome. You'll feel as though you are dining in an atmosphere of regal splendor. The rich, colorful decor is enhanced by sparkling crystal and beautiful tableware.

The Astra Dome dining car where superlative meals are served.

The luxurious main dining car on the lower level.

Sleeper-lounge observation car *La Mirada*, built for Rock Island's *Golden Rocket*. The postwar interior of this feature car for the proposed Chicago–Los Angeles train reflects the "home of the future" look, with just a few touches of traditional woodwork. Unusual touches included real plants behind glass windows and on the surfaces of seating dividers. Two sets of equipment were to be built for this train, one for Rock Island and the other for co-operator Southern Pacific. SP backed out of the *Golden Rocket* project before its set was constructed, but Rock Island's *Golden Rocket* cars were delivered and dispersed to upgrade existing trains; *La Mirada* became a fixture on the Rock Island-Southern Pacific's Chicago–Los Angeles streamliner *Golden State*. ILLUSTRATION BY MITCH MARKOVITZ

An entire *Daylight* was resurrected early in the 1980s for special excursion service. En route from Portland, Oregon, to New Orleans in May 1984 for the World's Fair, this phoenix *Daylight* approaches Mount Shasta in Northern California, giving onlookers a glimpse of the *Shasta Daylight* era of the 1950s. MIKE SCHAFER

streamliner, the *Golden State*, was a latecomer (1947–48) on a route nearly devoid of scenery. It lacked the truly distinctive feature cars found on its peer trains, like the *City of Los Angeles*, and it would never have dome cars.

However, SP and Rock Island made a joint effort to launch a deluxe streamliner concurrent with the *Golden State*, a train that was to cash in on a fleet name—the *Rockets*—that had been popularized in regional service offered by the Rock Island since 1937 (chapter 6). The new *Golden Rocket* was to be a tri-weekly, high-speed coach-and-Pullman train with a coffee shop-bar-lounge

known as the "Fiesta Car" (complete with mock awnings in the coffee shop section) and a sleeper-lounge observation car with a barber shop.

SP suddenly backed out of the arrangement just as the Rock Island-owned *Golden Rocket* trainset was completed, and SP never took delivery of its set of equipment. Rock Island simply reassigned its *Golden Rocket* cars—including the sleeper-lounge observation car *La Mirada*—to other trains, mainly the *Golden State*. The *Golden State* was discontinued in 1968, but a few *Golden Rocket* cars continued in local services into the 1970s.

THE ART OF THE STREAMLINER

SOUTHERN PACIFIC'S MULTI-COLORED FLEET

Although Southern Pacific was an early partner with UP on the *City of San Francisco*, the SP's own long-distance streamliner initiative didn't really begin in earnest until the *Shasta Daylight* was inaugurated between Oakland, California, and Portland, Oregon, in April 1949. The *Shasta* was bedecked in Southern Pacific's vibrant red, orange, and black paint scheme also used on its regional *Daylight* trains. Each of the train's nine chair cars featured restful color schemes inspired by the Oregon Cascades such as Crater Lake blue, cedar red, and summit green. The *Shasta*'s lounge, the "Timberline Tavern," was inspired by a year-round resort of the same name on Mount Hood. Bar fronts featured wooden hand-carved renditions of Northwest animal life. But the scenery outside the window provided the real attraction, and the

Shasta with its oversized windows in each car was well equipped for viewing the Cascades. In 1955, a full-length dome lounge car was also added. PA-type passenger diesels built by Alco (American Locomotive Company), readily acknowledged as the most attractive diesels ever built, often powered the beautiful train.

Though not designed for sightseeing, the *Shasta*'s overnight companion train on the same run, the *Cascade*, had its merits as well. Re-equipped with streamlined, two-tone gray equipment in 1950, this sleeping-car train boasted the most modern room accommodations available. Its centerpiece was an articulated triple-unit kitchen/diner/lounge car dubbed "Cascade Club," which offered more than 130 feet of formal dining room and lounge space. A semi-circular padded and chrome-trimmed bar was the focal point of an Art Deco interior.

Rather than hype the virtues of one specific train in a single ad, Southern Pacific took on all four of its newest streamliners—the *Sunset Limited, Golden State, Overland,* and *Shasta Daylight*—in this two-page ad from a 1951 issue of *Holiday* magazine. Note the "people waving at train" theme, always popular with railroad marketing departments. MIKE SCHAFER COLLECTION

Both the *Shasta* and *Cascade* eventually fell from grace as Americans abandoned streamliner travel for the auto and the airliner. The *Shasta* was discontinued in 1967 but the remnants of the *Cascade* evolved into Amtrak's extremely popular *Coast Starlight,* which operates over the route of both trains between Seattle and Los Angeles.

Another SP entry reborn about 1950 had its own personality and distinctive charm. Touted as "The Streamlined Train with the Southern Accent," the Budd-built, stainless-steel *Sunset Limited* between Los Angeles and New Orleans featured interior designs unique to New Orleans and the Southwest such as the "French Quarter Lounge" and the "Pride of Texas" coffee shop.

ZEPHYRS EXPAND

The excitement generated by the fleet of 1930s articulated Burlington *Zephyr* trainsets—from the three-car *Zephyr* 9900 to the 12-car *Denver Zephyr*—had been stymied by wartime manufacturing restrictions, but even before hostilities ended in 1944, the railroad and manufacturer Budd Company laid extravagant plans for a new fleet of stainless-steel passenger trains. In 1945, the Burlington tried out a new concept by rebuilding one of its prewar, Budd-built conventional streamlined coaches into a passenger car with an upper-level, glass-enclosed "bubble" viewing deck. The car was christened *Silver Dome* and dispatched on exhibition runs. Passengers loved the all-around view. Two years later, the Chicago-Twin Cities *Twin Zephyrs* were re-equipped with new Budd trainsets that included five "Vista-Domes" (as Budd called its production dome cars) per train. More rounded than their experimental predecessor, the new cars would become ubiquitous on many other *Zephyrs* to come. The die was cast: where overhead clearances per-

Riding the rails of the Western Pacific Railroad, the stainless-steel *California Zephyr* splices through the pine country of California's Feather River Canyon in July 1969. Orange-striped locomotives with red winged nose emblems made the oncoming train stand out against the earthy countryside. The train's five domes were key to its success. MIKE SCHAFER

LEFT: Lunch on the *California Zephyr* meant views from your dining table—like this one of Colorado's Byers Canyon. The whole CZ and its operation were geared around sightseeing. BOB JOHNSTON

A fixture aboard the pre-Amtrak *California Zephyr* was the "Zephyrette" train hostess, prominent in this CZ folder from the 1950s. JOE WELSH COLLECTION

mitted, domes would become a marquee item as railroads converted their entire passenger-train fleets into modern streamliners.

As the 1947 Vista-Dome *Twin Zephyr*s were being designed, the Burlington and its transcontinental partners of the heavyweight Chicago–Oakland/San Francisco *Exposition Flyer*—Western Pacific and Denver & Rio Grande Western—also placed an order for six sets of stainless-steel cars to be launched in March 1949 as the *California Zephyr,* which would replace the *Flyer.* Budd designer John Harbeson made a trip over the Burlington-Rio Grande-Western Pacific route in anticipation of his development of the *CZ*'s design. Marveling at Colorado's Rocky Mountains and California's Feather River Canyon, Harbeson confirmed that five dome cars on each of the six sets of *CZ* equipment was entirely appropriate for the first long-distance streamliner whose schedule was arranged expressly for sightseeing. Once passengers discovered the

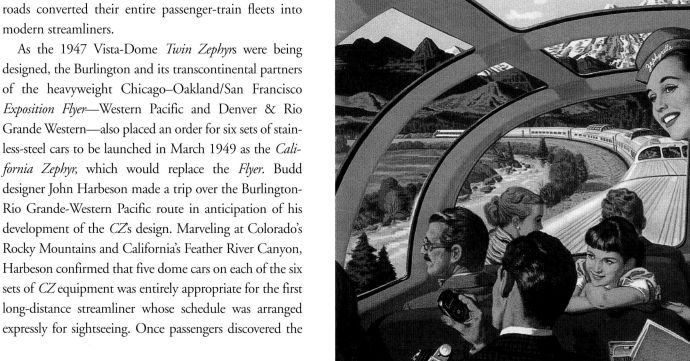

CHICAGO · SAN FRANCISCO
THE VISTA-DOME
California Zephyr

CHICAGO · SAN FRANCISCO
THE VISTA-DOME
California Zephyr

BURLINGTON · RIO GRANDE
WESTERN PACIFIC

BURLINGTON · RIO GRANDE
WESTERN PACIFIC

FACING PAGE, UPPER: *California Zephyr* sleeper-lounge observation car *Silver Planet* trails the eastbound CZ crossing above Colorado State Highway 72 near Plainview in 1969. The Vista-Dome sleeper-lounge observations were the most exotic cars in *California Zephyr* service; they were for the exclusive use of Pullman passengers. BOB JOHNSTON

RIGHT: If you were a Pullman passenger on the *California Zephyr*, you could ascend this golden staircase—illuminated by lucite rod handrails and miniature stair spotlights—in the sleeper-lounge-observation car to the Vista-Dome for an evening of star gazing or a day of mountain sightseeing. This view from the first-class lounge of car *Silver Crescent* (a sister car to that on the facing page) reflects the ambience of the landmark land-cruise train. The short staircase down leads to the under-dome bar and beyond to the bedrooms. Note the writing desk at far right, under wall art of the Golden Gate Bridge. JOHN FORBES MC CLEAN

FACING PAGE, LOWER: The front of the under-dome bar on the CZ's Vista-Dome sleeper-lounge observation car had intricate leather artwork. This is the bar in car *Silver Crescent*. JOHN FORBES MC CLEAN

experience, the scenic cruiseliner quickly became "the most talked-about train in America," both in advertising and in reality. Additional cars were ordered, and summer consists were swelled with extra sleepers and coaches.

Aside from the domes, this *Zephyr*'s innovations included recorded music piped into individual rooms, and hall windows opposite bedroom doors to allow occupants to view out both sides of the train. These subtleties went hand-in-hand with the more memorable touches: friendly "Zephyrette" hostesses to make passengers feel at home, fresh flowers in the dining car, and pastry fresh-baked on board. One of the dome cars on each equipment set was a buffet-lounge. Later these cars were remodeled into "Cable Car Room" lounges—with a Bay Area motif featuring scale-model cable cars and San Francisco murals. The sleeper observation car, with its orange neon tail sign and revolving red "Mars" light piercing the night, contained a single drawing room with an on-board shower—an uncommon feature at the time.

But the Burlington wasn't finished. Several years after the *CZ*'s equipment arrived, the railroad in 1956 re-equipped its Chicago–Denver flagship streamliner, the *Denver Zephyr*, with two new 14-car trains that combined speed and shiny elegance between the Windy and Mile-High cities (some cars continued beyond Denver to Colorado Springs), the last complete streamliners the Budd Company would build.

Targeting the overnight market, the *DZ*'s Vista-Dome parlor-lounge observation car showcased the "Colorado Room," complete with hand-painted murals of Rocky Mountain scenery; the mid-train Vista-Dome buffet-lounge was fashioned as the "Chuck Wagon" coffee shop, with a menu and informal ambience catering primarily to coach passengers. The *Denver Zephyr* now even had its own branding-iron design—a "D"-bar-"Z." In an attempt to snag additional riders, a new budget sleeping car, the Slumbercoach, offered narrower beds in more-compact rooms at lower prices. Though the cramped digs and smallish windows of the Slumbercoach were not exactly designed with the claustrophobic in mind, these cars were a hit with the budget-minded who wanted private room accommodations.

Since its inaugural in 1936, the *Denver Zephyr* was one of Burlington's most popular trains. The stainless steel still glistens on the 1956-built cars of the *DZ* departing Denver for Chicago in late summer 1971. Amtrak had taken over the train's operation by this time, but still operated the *DZ*'s equipment intact. MIKE SCHAFER

THE CZ'S CANADIAN COUSIN

The *California Zephyr's* popularity spawned a near look-alike stainless-steel transcontinental cruiseliner in Canada. Though Canadian Pacific's 1955 maroon-striped *Canadian* lacked the heavy complement of dome coaches, the train duplicated the *Zephyr's* silver panache in its feature Vista-Dome sleeper-lounge observation car, mid-train Vista-Dome buffet, and dining car. Murals of majestic peaks adorned the below-dome lounges, and etched glass partitions added a touch of elegance to the diners. Originally operating daily from its twin eastern termini of Toronto and Montreal to Vancouver, British Columbia,

via Banff, Alberta, the *Canadian* offered seven types of sleeping accommodations including the last major order of sleepers containing open sections ever built. Though its routing and ownership has changed over the years as passenger train operation was passed from the CP to Canada's VIA Rail, the original *Canadian* equipment remains the only North American streamliner to survive essentially intact into the twenty-first century. Today the stripes are blue, but thanks to a top-to-bottom refurbishment program undertaken by VIA in the 1980s and 1990s, you can still ride the *Canadian* today between Toronto and Vancouver (via Jasper).

ABOVE: The *California Zephyr's* northern cousin, the *Canadian,* winds through Kicking Horse Pass in British Columbia's Yoho National Park in 1972. MIKE SCHAFER

INSET: Passengers in the *Canadian's* diner ate under a canopy of "stars." BOB JOHNSTON COLLECTION

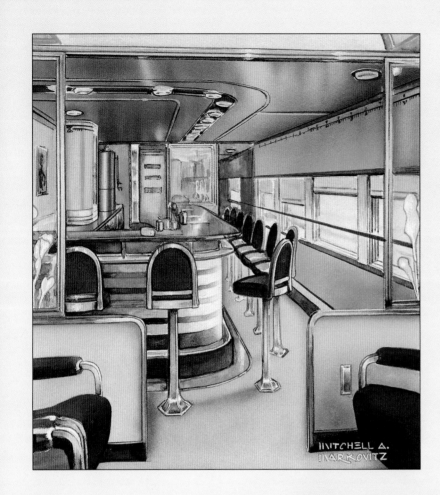

PACIFIC NORTHWEST FLEET

The Great Northern and Northern Pacific railroads each had long-established trains from Chicago through the Twin Cities to Seattle and Portland that needed a facelift, and both railroads took the parallel approach of launching lightweight trains in the 1940s and further re-equipping them in the 1950s with domes and lounge cars. The smooth-sided streamlined versions of GN's *Empire Builder* and the NP's *North Coast Limited* initiated a departure from the staid, solid color palette of their heavyweight predecessors.

Locomotive manufacturer EMD and Pullman designers went with an eye-catching combination of orange and dark green bands accented with yellow striping for the *Builder*, with the train name prominently displayed in a distinctive Art Deco typeface on the top of every car. Inside, extensive use was made of murals depicting scenes of the countryside through which the train traveled and North American Indian themes. Joining the *Builder's* pool of rolling stock in 1951, "The Ranch" provided a wood-paneled, pinto-leather-seat coffee shop for lighter meals; the railroad's initials were displayed overhead like a

ENROUTE ON
The Incomparable
EMPIRE BUILDER

ABOVE: The interior colors of the lunch counter-lounge of the 1947 *Empire Builder* mimicked those of the outside terrain, and the stripes on the lunch counter itself mirrored Native American design elements. Cold sandwich with lettuce and mayonnaise and the crusts trimmed off, anyone? ILLUSTRATION BY MITCH MARKOVITZ

RIGHT: The lunch counter-lounge of the 1951 *Builder* was called "The Ranch" and featured rustic décor and the train's own branding iron. PHILLIP R. HASTINGS, M.D., COLLECTION, CALIFORNIA STATE RAILROAD MUSEUM

corral moniker on a simulated rustic fence. When Budd-built Vista-Domes arrived in 1955, the new train's centerpiece and social center became the "Great Dome" (on the bridge in the above photo) and provided scenic viewing for the full length of this 85-foot-long car on top and a colorful lounge with totem-pole decor underneath.

Pullman's first streamlined *North Coast Limited* color scheme was updated in 1951 by designer Raymond Loewy, who came up with a stunning two-tone green treatment showcasing the NP's monad trademark in the center of each car below the window line. After Budd Vista-Dome coaches and unique dome sleeping cars were added in 1954, the slogan "Vista-Dome *North Coast*

ABOVE: In the late 1960s, the Great Northern went through an image change that included a new paint scheme—dubbed "Big Sky Blue"—intended for all its freight and passenger diesels and passenger rolling stock. In this scene of the *Empire Builder* in Glacier Park, Montana, in the summer of 1968, the old look is giving way to the new. BOB JOHNSTON

RIGHT: In this impressionistic artwork on a 1966 train folder, the Chicago–Seattle *Western Star* still wears GN's celebrated green-and-orange paint scheme. BOB JOHNSTON COLLECTION

★ It's great going on the ★
western star
Great Northern's fast, modern transcontinental train

GREAT NORTHERN RAILWAY

"Traveller's Rest" for which this de luxe car was named, was a favorite campsite of explorers Lewis and Clark

ABOVE: Passengers aboard NP's *North Coast Limited* could write home on one of these postcards available on the train. The postcard scene shows the stewardess-nurse of the *North Coast Limited* holding court in the Travelers' Rest lounge, showing passengers the route followed by the two famous explorers on a large map on the wall. MIKE SCHAFER COLLECTION

TOP RIGHT: Industrial designer Raymond Loewy developed Northern Pacific's eye-pleasing two-tone green color scheme. BOB JOHNSTON

Olympian Hiawathas

HIAWATHA LOUNGE COACH · · · 1947 STYLE

Limited' bracketed the monad. A year later, the Lewis & Clark Traveler's Rest lounge cars answered the GN's Ranch car with a dramatic, spotlit diorama sweeping up from wall to ceiling of the car with a painted map of the explorers' route, closely traversed by the train, accompanied by water color drawings of scenes the party likely encountered. Describing the perils of the early adventurers was a registered stewardess-nurse, who also provided medical assistance, if needed. New dining cars with bright interiors and etched-glass partitions were introduced in 1958; today, the two-tone green is gone, but some of the *North Coast* diners have been completely updated into combination dining and coffee shop cars and are still rolling under the Amtrak banner (chapter 7).

Unlike the Great Northern and Northern Pacific's Chicago–Pacific Coast entries, The Milwaukee Road's *Olympian Hiawatha* consists benefited from homegrown

COMFORTABLE RECLINING CHAIRS IN THE RESTFUL AND ROOMY

Lounge Coaches

Your seat is a modern masterpiece orthopedically designed for restful support, and padded with luxurious foam rubber that literally keeps you floating on air.

THE MILWAUKEE ROAD has painted the lily by further improving the Hiawatha reclining seat lounge coaches. These airy, spacious cars are scientifically designed for maximum comfort in long distance travel. All seats are reserved.

Each chair is individually controlled, may be adjusted to a deep reclining position and has its own footrest. Fluorescent lights in the outer edge of the deep luggage racks diffuse even, glare-free illumination over all seats. The decorative scheme is varied with alternate cars having green and gold or gray and maroon upholstery, and beige or gray wall panels of linen-finish plastic.

The separate lounging rooms for men and women in the 1947 Hiawatha coaches are exceptionally commodious and provide ample space for dressing and lounging. Each lounge is appropriately decorated with colorful prints by well-known artists and designers.

ABOVE: The hallmark diesels of Milwaukee Road's *Olympian Hiawatha* were masterpieces of Art Deco, bedecked with chrome nose shields. They were built by Fairbanks-Morse, of Beloit, Wisconsin, with help from General Electric in Erie, Pennsylvania. MILWAUKEE ROAD HISTORICAL ASSOCIATION ARCHIVES

LEFT: Milwaukee Road spared no expense in producing a promotional booklet for its new *Olympian Hiawatha*. In the interior scene on the facing page, note the unusual wall pattern in the window area, done with a combination of wood veneer and paint. Detailed floorplans familiarized passengers with each car of the exotic train. JOE WELSH COLLECTION

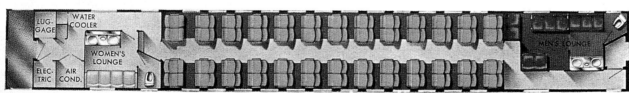

Each OLYMPIAN HIAWATHA *coach seats 52 in the body of the car. Air conditioning is of an advanced type, and there is an electric water cooler.*

LEFT: Designed by Brooks Stevens, the Sky Top sleeper-lounge observation car of the *Olympian Hiawatha* was unlike any other tail car (save for the Chicago–Twin Cities *Hiawatha*s). The car presented unusual engineering and structural challenges with its multi-paned window panels, nearly all of which were of different shapes and sizes. Together they formed a stunning canopy of glass from which to view the Rocky Mountains and Cascade Range. ILLUSTRATION BY MITCH MARKOVITZ

RIGHT: Milwaukee Road's Sky Top observation cars were as interesting outside to look at as they were inside the glassed-in solarium area. For designer Brooks Stevens, the structural design of the car end was a test of geometric skills. ALVIN SCHULTZE

streamliner know-how that dated from the steam-powered Chicago–Twin Cities *Hiawatha* of the 1930s. While Pullman and Budd designers were cranking out variations on their companies' standard lightweight coach, sleeper, lounge, and dining cars, the Milwaukee turned to local design visionary Brooks Stevens and Milwaukee Road shop forces. The team's greatest triumph was the rakish, bullet-end Skytop observation car, which was the first tail car to feature rows of overhead glass panels on all sides. The first Skytops appeared on the 1948 *Twin Cities Hiawatha*s, and Pullman-Standard built the sleeper versions for the *Olympian Hiawatha* in 1949. *Olympian Hi* diners had rounded interior walls sloping up to hide indirect lighting in a rectangular clerestory, and a number of triangular tables for two gave the car an airy feel. Other Milwaukee Road touches included distinctive porthole windows at the end of each car and wood paneling in coaches, economy all-section Touralux sleepers, and the Tip Top Tap lounge-coffee shop car.

Mid-train sleeping cars delivered by Pullman in 1949 were standard issue, but they still sported the distinctive porthole window treatment. Full-length Super Domes beat the GN *Empire Builder*'s Great Domes to the punch by three years in 1952. Up front for a short time after the *Olympian Hi* debuted in 1947 were chrome-fronted Fairbanks-Morse passenger diesels with the name of the train emblazoned on their orange, maroon, and gray flanks. Streamlined "Little Joe" or big boxy bi-polar electric locomotives took over for almost 700 miles of electrified territory in Montana and the state of Washington. All of these idiosyncratic trappings helped the *Olympian Hiawatha* to exude its railroad's pride from the moment passengers stepped aboard. It was, perhaps, the last glimmer of design individualism of the mid-century streamlined era, crowded out by the mass-produced rolling stock from the Budd and Pullman-Standard factories. Alas, economically if not artistically, the train couldn't successfully compete on the last Pacific Northwest transcontinental line to be completed and flickered out prematurely before the heavy summer travel season in 1961. The Milwaukee went bankrupt almost 20 years later, and tracks were pulled up over much of the route shortly thereafter.

When Milwaukee Road introduced Super Domes to the *Olympian Hiawatha* and other trains in 1952, the railroad gave the new cars widespread publicity. The "people waving at the train and train passengers waving back" theme that was all the rage in postwar passenger-train promotion was applied to this calendar art of the *Olympian Hiawatha* winding through a precipitous canyon. JOE WELSH COLLECTION

ST. PAUL

MINNEAPOLIS

ROCHESTER

WINONA

WYEVILLE

MANKATO

THE
400

5001

CHICAGO AND NORTH WESTERN

MA

ROUTE OF THE
REAMLINERS AND CHALLENGERS
TO *THE WEST*

The expanse of Chicago & North Western's regional "400" streamliner fleet is colorfully illustrated in this pre-World War II aerial perspective map. MIKE SCHAFER COLLECTION

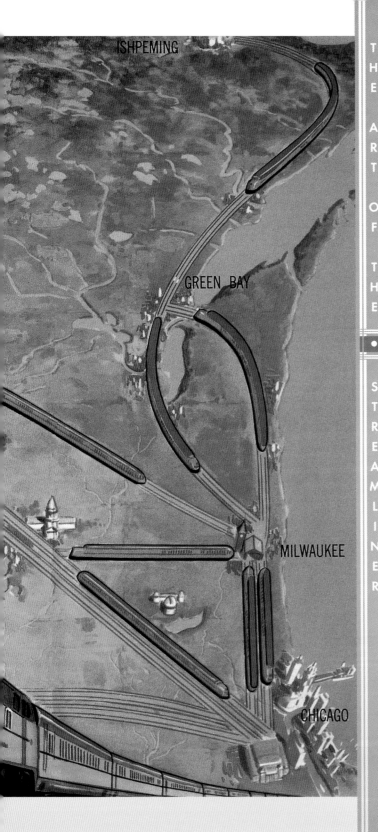

ISHPEMING

GREEN BAY

MILWAUKEE

CHICAGO

REGIONAL SPECIALTIES

STREAMLINING THE SHORT-HAULS

The original streamlined speedsters of the 1930s spawned fleets of regional trains that often traded on the name recognition—and excitement—generated by the originator of each breed. With locomotives and passenger cars being produced by only a handful of manufacturers, successfully developing brand loyalty through uniform exterior paint, interior design, marketing brochures, and advertisements could conceivably tilt customer preferences enough to improve ridership and revenue on trains that would otherwise remain faceless. Like packages in a grocery store competing with each other for shelf space, railroads hoped brands such as *Zephyr*, *Hiawatha*, *"400"*, and *Rocket* would elicit not only thoughts of "speed and comfort," but also "good food," "friendly staff," "clean" and, hopefully, "on-time" when potential travelers were considering how to get from here to there. Regional streamliners included an enormous variety of approaches to design and service, represented here by just a few—but colorful—samples.

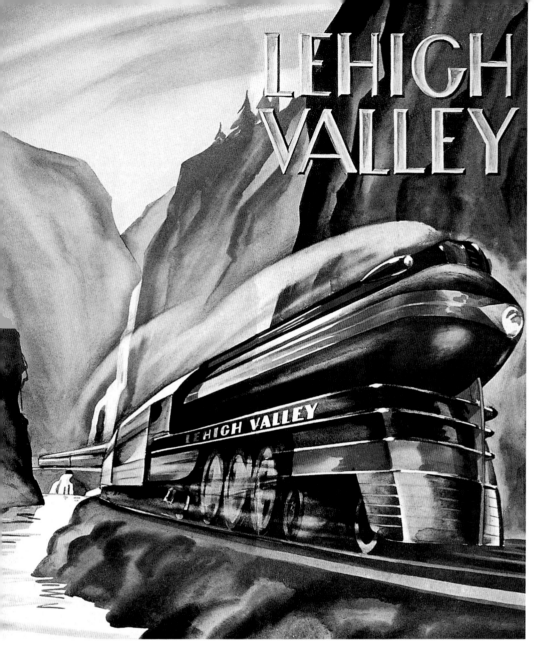

LEHIGH VALLEY

The *John Wilkes* diner had curtain dividers with a diamond-and-steam-train print pattern. Note the unusual above-window vertical lighting. LEHIGH VALLEY

The brochure for Lehigh Valley's new *John Wilkes* steam streamliner featured dynamic cover artwork by the train's designer, Otto Kuhler. JOE WELSH COLLECTION

STREAMLINERS ON A BUDGET

Emerging from the Great Depression, many smaller lines knew they needed to establish a streamliner brand to compete with the big roads, but barely had the financial wherewithal to do so. With little cash on hand in 1938, the Lehigh Valley turned to industrial designer Otto Kuhler for help. Kuhler's first creation was the *Asa Packer*, in reality a heavyweight train whose steam locomotive had only a sloping panel on the front carrying the train's name and modest skirting painted to

suggest speed. The train was painted black and orange, said to represent coal and the orange glow of a blast furnace. Encouraged by rave reviews from patrons, the Valley ventured further into the concept of streamlining with the June 1939 introduction of the *John Wilkes* on a run between New York and Wilkes-Barre/Pittston, Pennsylvania. Named for a famous defender of the American Colonies in the British Parliament, the train was largely the product of the railroad's shops at Sayre, Pennsylvania. Shop personnel were so proud of the work they'd done to execute the streamlined design on the older heavyweight equipment that each car contained a small plaque commemorating their efforts. Over seven tons of sheet metal was used to transform two 20-year old steam locomotives into sleek, bullet-nosed beauties finished in classy Cornell red and black with white striping. Behind the coal tender, lounge car *Anthracite Club* featured a cocktail bar; the diner was refitted with new tables, customized draperies, modern aluminum chairs, and fluorescent lighting. A year later, Kuhler completed his Lehigh Valley work by stylizing and streamlining the

Electroliners ARE HERE!

America's First All-Electric Luxury Trains

Five Trips Each Way—Every Day
Between Chicago and Milwaukee

Every ELECTROLINER coach is smartly styled by master designers in a different color motif— coral, blue and gold ... scarlet and gray ... apricot and turquoise. Separate smoking lounges, lens-control illumination, electric air-conditioning and temperature control give you luxury travel at its finest.

Enjoy a perfectly-served "snack" or refreshments in the unique Tavern-Lounge as you glide smoothly over the rails. With its clever murals, its superb appointments, its specially-designed lighting, the distinctive Tavern-Lounge is festive, colorful and inviting! All ELECTROLINER interiors styled and created by James F. Eppenstein and Associates.

Thrill to an entirely new experience in smooth-flowing travel on swift, silent ELECTROLINERS— the North Shore Line's incomparable new "trains of the future".... in service today!

Here are trains with ultra-modern appointments, luxurious equipment and club-like atmosphere unsurpassed in railroad service. Down to the last minute detail, every facility of the ELECTROLINERS is designed to give you *all-luxury* travel— at regular coach fares—on *all-electric* trains, electrically operated even to temperature control and electro-pneumatic brakes.

RIDE CUSHIONED IN RUBBER!... Nothing has been spared to make the new ELECTROLINERS a triumph in riding comfort. Sweep along easily, silently in spacious *all-electric* trains, completely insulated and sound-proofed to keep out noises .... electrically air-conditioned and heated .... and "cushioned in rubber" at every possible point to give a matchless, quiet, smooth-flowing ride.

NEVER BEFORE TRAINS LIKE THESE! Deep-upholstered seats .... separate smoking lounges .... superbly equipped Tavern-Lounge Cars with softly cushioned settees and unique refreshment appointments .... here indeed is high-speed, all-electric luxury travel .... the first of its kind in America.

ABOVE: A Chicago North Shore & Milwaukee timetable from 1941 featured art that showed off the colorful interiors of the railroad's new Chicago–Milwaukee *Electroliners*. MIKE SCHAFER COLLECTION

RIGHT: Riding a Milwaukee-bound train, the photographer aimed his camera out the rear window at a Chicago-bound *Electroliner* on 6th Street in Milwaukee in late summer 1962. The *Electroliners* had crew cabs at both ends to obviate turning the trains at terminals. BOB JOHNSTON

TOP RIGHT: *Electroliner* theming carried through in the diner, where menus replicated the train's noses and patrons ate off of tan *Electroliner* china—on lightning-bolted placemats. This scene is aboard the restored '*Liner* at the Illinois Railway Museum. MIKE SCHAFER

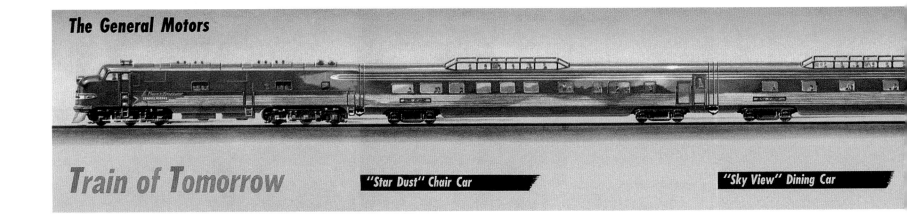

The General Motors

Train of Tomorrow

"Star Dust" Chair Car

"Sky View" Dining Car

A collaboration of diesel-builder Electro-Motive and carbuilder Pullman-Standard, the 1947 *Train of Tomorrow* predicted that the postwar streamliner would be "domeliners." In several cases, they weren't far off. The dome-studded *Train of Tomorrow* toured the U.S. for three years, and many promotional folders and brochures were distributed to the public. This pocket-size paper promotion unfolded to show the locomotive and each of the train's named cars. MIKE SCHAFER COLLECTION

FACING PAGE: In another, larger promotional piece, each *Train of Tomorrow* car got special treatment, with interior renderings and descriptive copy. This page focused on dome-lounge observation car *Moon Glow*. The cut-away illustrated how the dome section tied into the rest of the car. MIKE SCHAFER COLLECTION

road's flagship, the New York–Buffalo *Black Diamond*, once again utilizing his trademark bullet nose on the steamers and the same handsome exterior and interiors that adorned the *John Wilkes*. The *Black Diamond*'s train attendants received new uniforms featuring red, black, and white trim and embroidered with the *Black Diamond* name.

At about the same time in the Midwest, a pair of smooth-sided "glorified streetcars" would help the Chicago North Shore & Milwaukee go toe-to-toe with streamliners launched by neighboring Chicago & North Western and Milwaukee Road. Built by the St. Louis Car Company in 1940, North Shore Line's twin *Electroliners* kept the 90-mile interurban line competitive with parallel C&NW and Milwaukee Road on the Chicago–Milwaukee corridor. St. Louis Car had special considerations in designing the trains. At the north end of the railroad in Milwaukee, the *Electroliners* trundled down city streets. In Chicago's Loop district at the south end of the run, they twisted through the city's tight-curved, narrow-platformed elevated structure. But, the trains also needed to scream down North Shore's Skokie Valley Line straightaway at nearly 90 MPH. The turquoise-and-coral, lightning-bolt-striped, four-car articulated electric interurban trains sprinted like jackrabbits while affording passengers a quiet, air-conditioned ride in coach seating or a dining car that served light snacks and beverages. Each train made two and a half round trips each day at just less than two hours for a one-way trip. Though the electric line ceased operation in 1963, the *Electroliners* lived on in

Philadelphia commuter service for more than a decade as the *Liberty Liner*s and today reside in Illinois and Pennsylvania museums as, along with a few other shapely pioneers, living tributes to the dawn of the streamlined era.

FILLING THE VOID

Attempting to capitalize on pent-up demand for new passenger rolling stock after World War II, General Motors and Pullman-Standard designers cooked up a four-car prototype known as the *Train of Tomorrow*, launched in 1947. Inspiration for the train's "Astra Domes" came when GM official C.R. Osborn rode a diesel locomotive cab through the Rockies on a freight train in 1943. "People would pay $500 to see what the engineer sees," he told the engineer, and shortly after sketched his idea for a special viewing car on a piece of paper. He shared this idea with Burlington President Ralph Budd, and in 1945 Burlington built the first dome car at its Aurora, Illinois, shops. The *Train of Tomorrow* expanded the concept, featuring the first dome diner and the first dome over a sleeping car. Initially sporting wrap-around stainless-steel sheathing from its custom locomotive down the length of the train to a chrome "bumper" that hid the coupler on the round-end lounge observation car, this one-of-a-kind demonstrator train barnstormed the U.S., and thousands of people walked through its innovative cars for a glimpse of what postwar passenger trains might be all about. After a three-year, 65,000-mile tour, the *Train of Tomorrow* was purchased by Union Pacific, which repainted it Armour yellow and gray and ran it in Seattle–Portland service.

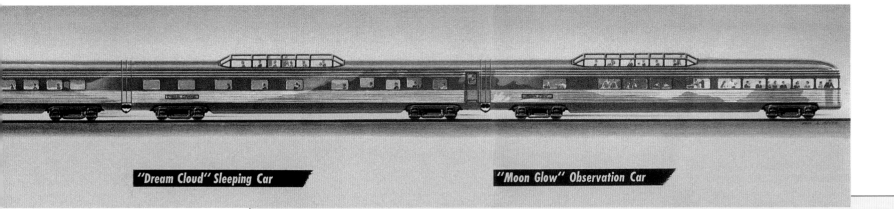

"Dream Cloud" Sleeping Car   "Moon Glow" Observation Car

One of the railroads apparently impressed with crowd reaction to the *Train of Tomorrow* was the Wabash, which promptly ordered a complete "domeliner" from the Budd Company. Four of the *Blue Bird*'s six cars—three coaches and a parlor-lounge observation car—had domes, making it look quite like the *Train of Tomorrow.* Competing directly against Illinois Central's recently re-equipped *Daylight* streamliner and Gulf, Mobile & Ohio's *Abraham Lincoln,* the *Blue Bird* upped the ante on the hotly contested Chicago–St. Louis market by being not only the first (and only, it would turn out) pre-Amtrak train to offer domes on that route, but also one of the first to offer Heywood-Wakefield "Sleepy Hollow" revolving, reclining seats. Each car featured murals painted by artist Auriel Bessemer in oils on canvas attached to bulkhead walls (can you imagine this in a train today?). The murals depicted aspects of life—both historic and contemporary—in the territory served by the *Blue Bird.* Interior colors on walls and drapery, not surprisingly, incorporated various shades of blue. Carpet patterns and colors varied from car to car. Overall, the décor was the work of the Wabash passenger and mechanical departments in collaboration with John Harbeson, of *Zephyr* 9900 (and other streamliners) fame.

Demand for parlor-car seating required Wabash to purchase an additional dome parlor car, but because the

Moon Glow observation car

A car for your leisure hours en route.
Nothing has been overlooked that might contribute toward
your enjoyment of the trip. The observation compartment in the
rear affords a magnificent view of the swiftly changing landscape, through
wide picture windows. There are two cocktail lounges, furnished much like
their counterparts in the smart supper clubs and hotels.
A writing desk occupies a semi-private nook; telephone service
is available to your home or business.

Never before such observation
in an observation car.

The gaily decorated cocktail lounge —
for relaxation and refreshment en route.

Budd Company was backed up with car orders for other railroads, Wabash had it built by Pullman-Standard. The smooth-sided car contrasted with the rest of the train's stainless-steel fluting, but it gave Wabash the extra revenue seating necessary—and with a bonus. The car featured a semi-private, under-dome lounge area known as the "Blue Bird Room."

Michigan's Pere Marquette Railway had also purchased cars from Pullman-Standard for its new Detroit–Grand Rapids *Pere Marquette*s. Though they arrived in 1946 before the dome craze was in full swing, the trains were

RIGHT: A colorized portrait of the Wabash *Blue Bird* taken at Forest Park near downtown St. Louis (the buildings have been airbrushed out of the background) graces a playing card from a deck sold in the train's lounge car. MIKE SCHAFER COLLECTION

BELOW: Parlor seating on the *Blue Bird*, which became a Norfolk & Western train after a 1964 merger with Wabash, featured swivel parlor chairs in alternating blue and mauve. MIKE SCHAFER COLLECTION

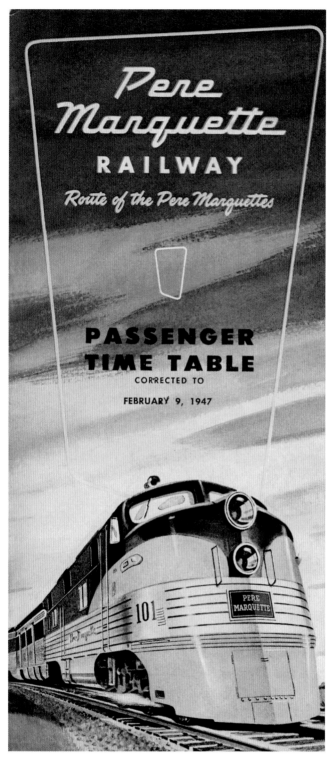

The Pere Marquette Railway produced a splashy public timetable to call attention to its new 1946 regional streamliners, the *Pere Marquettes*—the first new streamliners to go into service after World War II. MIKE SCHAFER COLLECTION

among the first to incorporate triangular tables in the dining car and to employ waitresses—as opposed to waiters—to serve the customers. Because the train was designed to shuttle back and forth without being turned around at the end of each run, both *Pere Marquette* trainsets had a coach-lounge observation car at each end bracketing two full coaches and a diner. A wave pattern sweeping up over the locomotive's nose cheeks and front wheels was reminiscent of the paint treatment first used on Illinois Central's *City of Miami*, and the lower locomotives sides were painted to simulate fluted stainless steel, thereby matching the actual stainless steel side panels of the cars that trailed.

The *Pere Marquettes* received new parlor cars in 1950 after the line had been absorbed by the Chesapeake &

TOP: The Chicago-bound *Pere Marquette* at Hartford, Michigan, in 1966 still has travel appeal with its cheery yellow, blue, and gray/stainless-steel livery. Chesapeake & Ohio took over the the Pere Marquette in 1947. WILLIAM T. CLYNES

ABOVE: The *Pere Marquettes* emphasized that patrons would be served by waitresses rather than waiters. Wreaths on the wall indicate this to be a holiday trip aboard the *Pere Marquette* for the photographer in the mid-1960s. Note the triangular two-seat tables on the right. BOB JOHNSTON

Ohio in 1947. In addition, the *Pere Marquettes* were the beneficiaries of some of the equipment that the Budd company had built in 1948 for C&O's planned Washington–Cincinnati *Chessie* streamliner, which was never launched. The influx of these extra cars allowed C&O to expand *Pere Marquette* service into a fleet that also served Saginaw and Muskegon, Michigan, and Chicago. For a time, in fact, some *Pere Marquette* runs sported former *Chessie* dome-coach observation cars, bringing the domeliner concept to the State of Michigan after all.

HIGH SPEED IN THE CENTRAL U.S.

When the Chicago & North Western instituted a deluxe new, high-speed, heavyweight steam-powered Chicago–Minneapolis run in 1935, the name *"400"* was chosen for the train's ability to travel 400 miles in about as many minutes. The moniker not only made the transition to the yellow-and-green streamlined equipment that replaced it in 1939, but also to streamlined trains on much slower routes that could achieve mile-a-minute timings only in a dream. Still, the indelible image of the speedometer in the rear lounge-observation car of the *Twin Cities "400"* flirting with 100 MPH was good enough to help differentiate trains like the *Dakota "400"* (Chicago–Huron, South Dakota),

BELOW: Colorized linen postcards from the 1940s showed the smart interiors of Chicago & North Western's "400" on the Chicago–Twin Cities route. Rich but earthy reds and greens on dining-car chairs, carpeting, and draperies nicely complemented the pastel greens and rose used on the walls. The coach scene shows an increasingly popular amenity on streamliners of the era: a stewardess or train hostess. BOTH, MIKE MC BRIDE COLLECTION.

THE NEW STREAMLINER "400" — CHICAGO AND NORTH WESTERN LINE

COLORFUL DINING ROOM ON NORTH WESTERN'S NEW "400"   9A-H1863

THE NEW STREAMLINER "400" — CHICAGO AND NORTH WESTERN LINE

COACHES ON THE NEW "400" ARE A REVELATION IN COMFORT AND BEAUTY   9A-H1862

The "400" (later known as the *Twin Cities* "400" to differentiate the Chicago–Twin Cities train from newer members of the fleet) wore a simple but effective color scheme of "English Stagecoach Yellow" and dark green. It's August 25, 1962, as the Minneapolis-bound *Twin Cities* "400" pulls away from Milwaukee's lakefront station. Within a year, the train would be gone, a victim not only of the burgeoning private automobile and air-travel industry, but competing *Zephyrs* and *Hiawathas* of the Burlington and Milwaukee Road. Both of those roads could boast domed trains and better scenery. BOB JOHNSTON

BOTTOM: In 1958, Chicago & North Western re-equipped selected "400" runs, putting them on "stilts." Thanks in part to the success of Santa Fe's Hi-Level equipment, North Western subscribed to the practicalities of bilevel train design, and its new 1958 trains were double deck. In this 1964 photo at the northern Wisconsin burgh of Eland (where even the depot has been painted in streamliner colors), the bilevel *Flambeau "400"* pauses for passengers en route to Chicago. BOB JOHNSTON

BELOW: Prior to entering regular service, the new bilevel cars were put on exhibition. The lounge car of the *Peninsula "400"* reveals an ultra-modern interior. The gallery-style open upper level is partially visible at upper left. JIM NEUBAUER

Flambeau "400" (Chicago–Ashland, Wisconsin), and *Peninsula "400"* (Chicago–Ishpeming, Michigan) from the milk runs that often plied the same routes. In 1958, the North Western re-equipped the *Flambeau "400"* and the *Peninsula "400"* with bilevel coaches, lounge cars, and parlor cars (diners were older single-level cars outfitted with false roofs to conform to the height of the bilevel equipment).

Similarly, Milwaukee Road's steam-powered *Hiawatha* between Chicago and the Twin Cities multiplied into diesel-powered *Morning* and *Afternoon Hiawatha*s on the same route, the *Chippewa-Hiawatha* to Upper Michigan, and the *Midwest Hiawatha* to Omaha, Nebraska, and Sioux Falls, South Dakota. Well into the 1950s, these secondary streamliners usually featured a full dining car or café and first-class parlor-car seats, either overstuffed chairs in a separate lounge or individual rotating easy chairs. Often, these trains received unique hand-me-downs from earlier in the streamliner era. For example, the "Beaver-Tail Drawing Room Parlor Car" that once

graced the rear of the original (1935) *Hiawatha* wound up on the *Midwest Hiawatha* when that train was inaugurated in 1940, the Twin Cities run having since been re-equipped.

Burlington's *Zephyr*s proliferated because the speedy stainless-steel image of the *Pioneer Zephyr* (*Zephyr* 9900) had been indelibly burned into everyone's mind, then evolved with every iteration of the *Twin, Denver,* and *California Zephyr*s to mean "Vista-Domes," "silver," and "fast." Thus, the railroad unfurled a host of *Zephyr*s: *Nebraska, Ak-Sar-Ben* (Nebraska spelled backward), *Kansas City, Silver Streak, American Royal,* and the like.

Another memorable Midwest and South Central U.S. streamlined institution was Chicago, Rock Island & Pacific's *Rocket* fleet, which in 1937 began linking such

ABOVE: Milwaukee Road's *Hiawatha* observation cars were always a departure from the more-traditional round-end cars found on most other streamliners. The Beaver Tail (so-called account of its flat, sloping back end) parlor observation cars built for the 1938 edition of the *Twin Cities Hiawatha* were arguably the most distinctive (at least until the Skytop cars of 1948). Fins above the large rear viewing windows put these cars in the realm of Buck Rogers. Is this the train to La Crosse, or a spaceship? MILWAUKEE ROAD HISTORICAL ASSOCIATION ARCHIVES

ABOVE LEFT: The interior of the 1938 Beaver Tail cars featured Art Deco touches that complemented the car's distinctive exterior. The armrests of the lounging chairs facing out the rear windows were strong Art Deco statements as was the table lamp on the back of the outward-facing love seat at the very rear of the car. Note, too, the arrows on the windowed dividers. Nearly all streamlined cars for the *Hiawatha* fleet were built at the railroad's famous Milwaukee Shops, which allowed the Milwaukee to construct cars that were markedly different from those manufactured by the major carbuilders. MILWAUKEE ROAD HISTORICAL ASSOCIATION ARCHIVES

ABOVE: In the 1948 *Twin Cities Hiawatha*, designer Brooks Stevens used plenty of glass to create a breathtaking solarium area in the Sky Top parlor-lounge observation car. Because of a war-related shortage of curved glass, Stevens relied on a complex combination of flat window panes in the design. This view shows sunlight streamlining into one of the famous cars on the *Afternoon Hiawatha* in 1970. JIM HEUER

RIGHT: It appears that most *Hiawatha* passengers in this 1968 scene have deserted the Sky Top in favor of parallel Interstate 94. BOB JOHNSTON

ABOVE: Burlington's 1947 Budd-built *Twin Zephyrs* were perhaps the epitome of post-war train design, right down to their fluted-side Electro-Motive E5 diesels—with nose markings mimicking an early shovel-nose *Zephyr*. At Oregon, Illinois, in 1963, the Minneapolis-bound *Morning Zephyr*, though short two domes on this day (five were the norm), accelerates away from the depot. JIM BOYD

RIGHT: Budd domes would find new life on Amtrak trains. This refurbished car is on the *City of New Orleans* in 1992. BOB JOHNSTON

ROUTE OF THE *Rockets*

THE PEORIA-CHICAGO STREAMLINED ROCKET

A *Peoria Rocket* postcard from the late 1930s illustrates Rock Island's vibrant paint scheme, designed by General Motors. MIKE SCHAFER COLLECTION

R O C K   I S L A N D   L I N E S

city pairs as Chicago and Peoria, Illinois; Chicago and Des Moines, Iowa; Fort Worth and Houston, Texas; and Minneapolis/St. Paul and Kansas City. In 1939, the *Rocket* fleet also evolved into a long-distance service with the introduction of the *Rocky Mountain Rocket* between Chicago and Denver and Colorado Springs, and the *Twin Star Rocket* between Minneapolis and Houston. Distinctive red-and-maroon locomotives powered the stainless-steel *Rocket* fleet.

Nearby, the original lightweight Missouri Pacific *Eagle* first flew along the Missouri River between St. Louis, Kansas City, and Omaha in 1940 with coaches, a diner-lounge, and observation parlor car (with radio) attired in a complex scheme—designed by Raymond Loewy and Electro-Motive—of blue and gray with silver and yellow stripes. As with the *Zephyr*s, *Hiawatha*s, *"400s",* and *Rocket*s, the *Eagle* branding spread to other routes and trains, both regional (such as the *Valley Eagle* between Houston and Brownsville, Texas) and long-distance (the *Texas Eagle* between St. Louis and various Texas points). One of the more interesting cars on the Texas streamliner

MISSOURI PACIFIC LINES
"A SERVICE INSTITUTION"

PROUDLY PRESENT
THE *Eagle*
WORLD'S FINEST DAY LIGHT TRAIN

LEFT: In an overdose of enthusiastic artwork, the original of which resides at the National Transportation Museum near St. Louis, eagles both real and mechanical soar along rivers and towns. Such was the cover of the brochure introducing Missouri Pacific's first *Eagle*, which operated between St. Louis and Omaha. JOE WELSH COLLECTION

BELOW: The *Texas Eagle* has just made its morning arrival at St. Louis Union Station in the late 1950s. Missouri Pacific's *Eagle* paint scheme is yet another example of the design talents of GM's Electro-Motive Division. ALVIN SCHULTZE

ABOVE: In a scene that embodies the California mystique of yore, Southern Pacific's new *Daylight* steams into Santa Barbara circa 1937. The stunning red, orange, and black colors of "the world's most beautiful train" (a statement difficult to contest), were the perfect complement to the train's earthy surroundings dominated by greens, tans, and browns. UNION PACIFIC MUSEUM COLLECTION

RIGHT: The *Daylight*'s drumhead was a masterpiece of neon work, like the train itself, done in red and orange. The winged sun was the *Daylight*'s own Art Deco logo. MIKE SCHAFER

THE ART OF THE STREAMLINER

was a "soda fountain" sleeper-lounge that had a blind end for end-of-train use. It had backlit artificial windows simulating a traditional observation solarium. In 1948 and 1952, some *Eagles* received "Planetarium Dome" cars.

STREAMLINING ALONG THE COASTS

Initially a partner with Union Pacific in the newly emerging world of streamliners (the 1936 *City of San Francisco*), Southern Pacific soon instituted a distinctive franchise of its own, the *Daylight*. Clad in an arresting red-and-orange livery, the first Los Angeles-bound *Daylight* steamed out of San Francisco in 1937 with a matching heavy-duty streamlined steam locomotive capable of pulling the long train over heavy grades on the route. Unabashedly proclaimed by SP as "the world's most beautiful train," the fleet expanded shortly before World War II to include a *Morning Daylight* and *Noon Daylight* on the L.A.–San Luis Obispo–San Francisco route and the *San Joaquin Daylight* between L.A. and San Francisco via Bakersfield. In 1949, the *Shasta Daylight* became the first (and only) long-distance *Daylight*, linking Oakland/San Francisco with Portland, Oregon. Although each train showcased varying interior decoration keyed to the route it traveled, all trains featured two- and three-car sets of articulated coaches, dining cars, and full-length lounges. In an interesting twist from articulation designs used on early U.S. streamliners, Pullman-Standard eliminated the bulkheads between the linked car sections and instead employed full car-width diaphragms to keep out the elements. Without bulkheads at the points of articulation, car interiors appeared extra long— up to 130 feet versus the more-standard 85 feet—and spacious.

The same year that the *Daylight* made its debut in the West, on the East Coast the Reading Railroad launched the all-stainless-steel *Crusader* between Philadelphia and Jersey City, a Budd-built streamliner offering a diner-lounge, two coaches, and two round-end coach observation cars, one at either end of the train (the train was not turned at its terminals). "Clad in Shining Armor" as early advertising put it, the *Crusader* was powered by a Pacific-type steam locomotive shrouded in stainless steel with blue markings. Reading's trademark diamond emblem, which paid homage to the road's bread and butter commodity (coal), adorned the nose. Eventually, Electro-Motive diesels replaced steam, and in 1964 the little five-car streamliner was sold to the Canadian National.

In a sense, the lightweight revolution in Northeast pre-dated the *Flying Yankee* of 1935 and *Comet* of the same year (chapter 2) by a year with the 1934 rollout of 205 "turtleback"-roofed, smooth-sided "American Flyer"

The *Daylight*'s neon drumhead was mounted on the outside rear of this handsome round-end parlor observation car, whose interior carried out the Art Deco theming. The entire *Daylight*, except for its streamlined steam locomotive, was a product of Pullman-Standard. UNION PACIFIC MUSEUM COLLECTION

created by the New Haven Railroad, carbuilder Pullman, and designer Walter Dorwin Teague. After World War II, New Haven ordered more than 200 more of these cars, configured not only as coaches and grill cars, but also lounges, parlors, diners, and observation cars. This army of cars allowed New Haven to elevate its principal trains—among them the New York–Boston *Merchants Limited* and *Yankee Clipper*—to streamliner status. Originally attired in conservative hunter green with stainless-steel sheathing, the new cars featured big picture windows and clean, simplistic interior decor, though with a slight Art Deco touch through the generous use of chrome trim in some of the feature cars. Distinctive in shape as well as color, all of the new cars except the sleepers sported curved skirting and rounded roof lines. In the mid-1950s, the cars acquired a new exterior attire of red-orange in place of the hunter green window stripe.

ABOVE: Reading Lines ventured into world of new streamliners only once. Its all-stainless-steel *Crusader*, built by the Budd Company in Philadelphia (a hub for the Reading Railroad), catered to business people destined for New York and Philadelphia. Here, the *Crusader* cruises along the Jersey Central main line in 1952. JOHN DZIOBKO

RIGHT: Pennsylvania Railroad's *Congressional* and *Senator* were also business-oriented trains, serving the Boston–New York–Philadelphia–Washington corridor. The trains' parlor car interiors sported a combination Colonial/patriotic motif. LAWRENCE WILLIAMS, JOE WELSH COLLECTION

Powered by a handsome new GE rectifier-electric locomotive, the joint New Haven-Pennsylvania Railroad *Colonial* sweeps through Darien, Connecticut, in 1957. A heavyweight Pennsy coach interrupts what would otherwise be an all-matching Budd equipment set. The New Haven locomotive sports the railroad's new-image paint scheme, designed by a Swiss artist. Thanks in part to the Connecticut Department of Transportation, the flashy orange, black, and white livery would endure into the twenty-first century in commemoration of the famous regional railroad that vanished into history in 1969. JIM SHAUGHNESSY

Presenting Our New Babies

Twelve Sets of Twins

RIGHT AND BELOW: One of the most intricate and fascinating streamliner-related promotional folders was that issued by Maine Central and Boston & Maine for their new Pullman-Standard trains of 1947. One side of the fold-out shows the outside of coach *Bobolink* and restaurant-lounge car *Merrymeeting* while the flip side shows cutaways that reveal car interiors. MIKE SCHAFER COLLECTION

Many New Haven cars found their way south of New York City on trains operated through to Washington, D.C., in conjunction with the Pennsylvania Railroad. In 1949, New Haven re-equipped the jointly operated *Colonial* with cars from its large 1949 delivery from Pullman-Standard. But the Pennsy's own streamlined Northeast Corridor entries wouldn't appear until March 17, 1952, when the elite, new *Morning* and *Afternoon Congressionals* between New York and Washington and the *Senator* between Boston and Washington were launched. Constructed of stainless steel by Budd and featuring Tuscan red letterboards and gold lettering, the new trains reflected the nation's patriotic leanings at the time. Inside, red, white, and blue were the colors of choice while murals and etched glass art reflected colonial themes. The curved bar fronts of the *Congressional's* lounge cars even

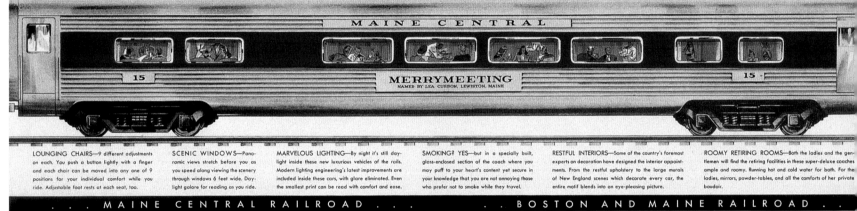

LOUNGING CHAIRS—9 different adjustments on each. You push a button lightly with a finger and each chair can be moved into any one of 9 positions for your individual comfort while you ride. Adjustable foot rests at each seat, too.

SCENIC WINDOWS—Panoramic views stretch before you as you speed along viewing the scenery through windows 6 feet wide. Daylight galore for reading as you ride.

MARVELOUS LIGHTING—By night it's still daylight inside these new luxurious vehicles of the rails. Modern lighting engineering's latest improvements are included inside these cars, with glare eliminated. Even the smallest print can be read with comfort and ease.

SMOKING? YES—but in a specially built, glass-enclosed section of the coach where you may puff to your heart's content yet secure in your knowledge that you are not annoying those who prefer not to smoke while they travel.

RESTFUL INTERIORS—Some of the country's foremost experts on decoration have designed the interior appointments. From the restful upholstery to the large murals of New England scenes which decorate every car, the entire motif blends into an eye-pleasing picture.

ROOMY RETIRING ROOMS—Both the ladies and the gentlemen will find the retiring facilities in these super-deluxe coaches ample and roomy. Running hot and cold water for both. For the ladies, mirrors, powder-tables, and all the comforts of her private boudoir.

. . . MAINE CENTRAL RAILROAD . . . . . BOSTON AND MAINE RAILROAD . . .

PORTER SERVICE—At no extra cost the Boston and Maine and the Maine Central will provide porter service for you in these new coaches. The porters and trainmen will be glad to help you stow away or to take down your baggage. Just ask and they will help you.

FOR YOUR BAGGAGE—Overhead you will find roomy baggage racks at each set of seats. The porters and trainmen will be glad to help you stow away or to take down your baggage. It's a convenient place to put those bags which you do not check.

SLEEP IF YOU WISH—You will find that each seat has an individual headrest and with the lounging comfort of the adjustable chairs it makes an ideal way to cat-nap while you speed along.

AIR-CONDITIONING—Naturally these new super-deluxe coaches are air-conditioned. Many new features and improvements are included in the air-cleaning and circulating equipment. Ideally warm and cozy in Winter, Spring and Fall. Comfortably cool in Summer with all temperature controls automatic.

LIST OF NAMES—You'll find the individual names of all the 24 new cars listed in this leaflet. The youngsters who named them are proud of these names and we are proud that 240,000 youngsters in Maine, New Hampshire, Vermont and Massachusetts entered the naming contest.

WE INVITE COMMENT—The seats are the famous "Sleepy Hollow" chairs, designed after Professor Hooten of Harvard University measured over 1,000 travelers in the North Station to secure the best specifications to make a coach seat ideally comfortable for the average traveler. If you have suggestions for improvements in our service we'll be glad to receive constructive criticism.

. . BOSTON AND MAINE RAILROAD . . . . . MAINE CENTRAL RAILROAD . . .

resembled a colonial military drum. Car names honored colonial heroes such as Paul Revere and Alexander Hamilton. Specially painted GG1 electric locomotives—the first appearance of Tuscan red on a GG1 in place of the usual Brunswick green—powered the trains between New York and Washington. In addition to parlor and coach seating, the *Congressional* offered a seven-room conference car designed to host business meetings en route. Parlor-bar observation cars brought up the rear of the trains, and a full dining car was available to patrons despite the fact that the *Congressional's* run lasted less than four hours. For those seeking a less formal setting, a coffee-shop car duplicated the medium-priced urban lunchroom of its time. After nearly two decades, the *Congressional* name would survive Amtrak's takeover of the nation's remaining intercity passenger operations in 1971; many *Congressional* cars were refurbished and could be seen at the end of the century in Northeastern service, notably on Amtrak's New York–Montreal *Adirondack* and the New York–Rutland, Vermont, *Ethan Allen Express.*

WHAT'S IN A NAME?

Though less remarked than the massive streamliner fleets of the New Haven, Pennsylvania, and other railroads across the country, a few lines chose the low-key approach to streamlining, but still did it with flair. A perfect example was the Boston & Maine and Maine Central, which quietly acquired 24 coaches, baggage coaches, and restaurant-lounge cars from Pullman-Standard in 1947 for their jointly-operated Boston–Bangor *Flying Yankee, Kennebec,* and *Pine Tree* trains (the original *Flying Yankee* streamliner of 1935 was reassigned elsewhere). They could have just

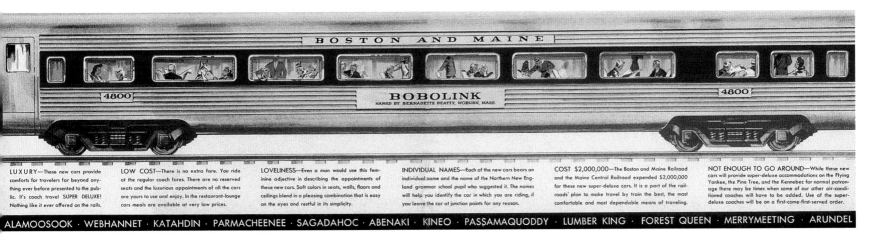

LUXURY—These new cars provide comforts for travelers far beyond anything ever before presented to the public. It's coach travel SUPER DELUXE! Nothing like it ever offered on the rails.

LOW COST—There is no extra fare. You ride at the regular coach fares. There are no reserved seats and the luxurious appointments of all the cars are yours to use and enjoy. In the restaurant-lounge cars meals are available at very low prices.

LOVELINESS—Even a man would use this feminine adjective in describing the appointments of these new cars. Soft colors in seats, walls, floors and ceilings blend in a pleasing combination that is easy on the eyes and restful in its simplicity.

INDIVIDUAL NAMES—Each of the new cars bears an individual name and the name of the Northern New England grammar school pupil who suggested it. The names will help you identify the car in which you are riding, if you leave the car at junction points for any reason.

COST $2,000,000—The Boston and Maine Railroad and the Maine Central Railroad expended $2,000,000 for these new super-deluxe cars. It is a part of the railroads' plan to make travel by train the best, the most comfortable and most dependable means of traveling.

NOT ENOUGH TO GO AROUND—While these new cars will provide super-deluxe accommodations on the Flying Yankee, the Pine Tree, and the Kennebec for normal patronage there may be times when some of our other air-conditioned coaches will have to be added. Use of the super-deluxe coaches will be on a first-come-first-served order.

ALAMOOSOOK · WEBHANNET · KATAHDIN · PARMACHEENEE · SAGADAHOC · ABENAKI · KINEO · PASSAMAQUODDY · LUMBER KING · FOREST QUEEN · MERRYMEETING · ARUNDEL

MEALS—On these new trains meals will be served in the Restaurant-Lounge car. Service for a snack or for an entire meal will be continuous. Prices will be consistently low, with everything priced so that we shall be able to serve only the best qualities of food.

DRINKS—Continuous service of beverages will be provided (liquor service consistent, of course, with State regulatory laws) in the dining section and in the lounge section.

LOUNGE—The lounge will be used for those who wish refreshments or, when the restaurant tables are fully occupied, by those who want a sandwich. Lounge seats will be free but must be kept for those who are eating or drinking.

QUIET OPERATION—The insulation in these cars embodies all the latest improvements for quiet, noiseless and vibrationless travel. You'll enjoy these new trains and we hope you find occasion to use them often.

STAINLESS STEEL—The car bodies are of light-weight alloy steel sheathed with stainless steel. They were built in New England by New England workmen. The seats were built by New England workmen.

TELL YOUR FRIENDS—If you like these new cars and the super-deluxe comforts they provide for travelers the dependable way in all sorts of weather, we'll appreciate your telling your friends about them. Comments or criticisms may be addressed to C. F. Palmer, Passenger Traffic Manager, North Station, Boston 14, Mass.

BOBOLINK · ROBIN · HUMMINGBIRD · BLACKBIRD · BLUEBIRD · ORIOLE · CHICKADEE · SNOWBIRD · PURPLE FINCH · BLUE JAY · BALD EAGLE · HERMIT THRUSH

The lounge area of the *Phoebe Snow*'s tavern-lounge observation car was partitioned off from the rest of the car through glass dividers, at left in this view. On the wall at the far end of the lounge area hung a portrait of Miss Snow. Car fixtures were otherwise standard items found in many Budd-built cars. BOB JOHNSTON

Truth in advertising was not yet an issue when Delaware, Lackawanna & Western issued this brochure for the new *Phoebe Snow* in 1949. The tavern-lounge observation car is prominent in this idealized scene in which the New York skyline seems to loom right at the head end of the train. In reality, the train terminated in Hoboken, across the Hudson River (about a mile wide at this point) from Manhattan. Travelers heading into the city had to utilize ferry boats or the Hudson & Manhattan rapid-transit line. JOE WELSH COLLECTION

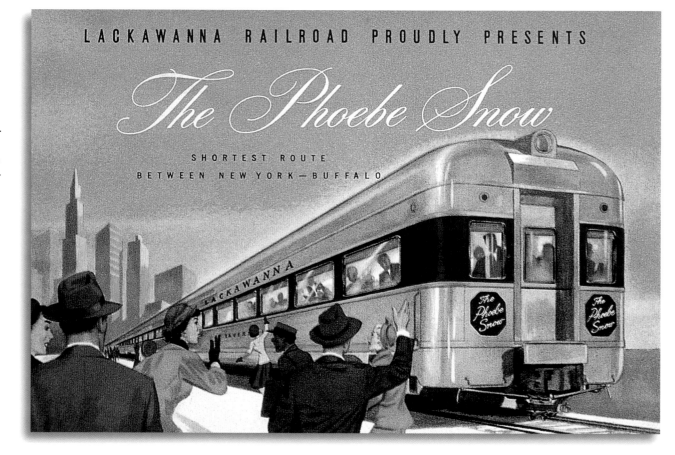

LACKAWANNA RAILROAD PROUDLY PRESENTS

The Phoebe Snow

SHORTEST ROUTE
BETWEEN NEW YORK — BUFFALO

numbered the coaches and blandly decorated the interiors, but instead the partners created colorful schemes with names to match. B&M's cars all had bird designations, while the Maine Central set drew from native Indian lore of the region and colorful function-specific names like *Merrymeeting* for a lounge car.

Another railroad, the Delaware, Lackawanna & Western, named a diesel-powered streamliner for a mythical woman. The *Phoebe Snow* had the distinction of having been built by three manufacturers: Pullman-Standard, American Car & Foundry, and Budd. Phoebe, who (as lore had it) often rode the Lackawanna between New York and Buffalo in the days of cinder-belching locomo-

tives, was no longer afraid to wear white because she "traveled the road of Anthracite." Though the hard, clean-burning anthracite coal did have its virtues, the railroad felt no remorse in retiring its steam engines when dieselization revolutionized American railroading after World War II. But when the Lackawanna placed into service a new maroon-and-gray streamliner over the Hoboken–Buffalo route in 1949, it tipped its hat to the past by naming the train *Phoebe Snow*. The railroad's longtime personification of clean, fast service was thus immortalized in the new train's smartly attired tavern-lounge observation car, where a portrait of her imagined nineteenth-century-era likeness hung on the wall.

Phoebe, now under the guidance of the Erie Lackawanna Railroad (formed by the 1960 merger of the DL&W and Erie railroads), skims across Slateford Viaduct over the Delaware River in western New Jersey, in December 1966. By this time, the *Phoebe Snow* had been extended all the way to Chicago. BOB JOHNSTON

Pausing under the moon in Philadelphia during 1999 testing, Amtrak's *Acela Express* heralded a new age in American streamlining. BOB JOHNSTON

RENAISSANCE STREAMLINING

⑦

THE STREAMLINER COMES BACK IN VOGUE

World War II interrupted America's streamliner boom in the 1940s, but the trend resumed with gusto—albeit in a more standardized, less individualistic fashion—after hostilities concluded. Then North America's railroads collectively began a battle against a new foe as they struggled to keep passenger trains financially viable in the face of heightened air and highway competition brought on by jet aircraft and the publicly financed interstate highway system. This competition prompted new approaches to streamlining in the 1950s, but these investments never paid off. The intercity passenger train nearly expired by the end of the 1960s, and finally in 1971 Amtrak was born to rescue the remains. After 50 years of increasing congestion on highways and airways, however, a growing public recognition that intercity passenger trains can play an increasingly vital role has led to a resurgence of investment in trains designed to generate excitement down at the station, just as the original streamliners of the 1930s once did.

The General Motors *Aerotrain* of 1956 represented yet another approach to streamlining. Utilizing super lightweight bus bodies from GM's motor-coach division and a futuristic locomotive body that hid a simple, modest (1200 hp), standard diesel power plant, GM sought to offer a new train that would be inexpensive to purchase and operate. Shown at Newark, New Jersey, this *Aerotrain* is testing on the Pennsylvania Railroad in 1956.
JOHN DZIOBKO

After World War II—but even before the 1950s took hold—American railroads suffered a shortfall in the projected ridership and revenues of their new streamliner fleets. An amazing number of new equipment orders had been placed with builders at war's end, but the railroads—much less anyone else—could not have predicted the extent of the boom that was about to embrace the automobile and airline industry. Nor were railroads ready for the soaring labor costs as well as general cost increases that would come.

Trains like Chesapeake & Ohio's *Chessie* and the Rock Island-Southern Pacific *Golden Rocket* were cancelled. Much of the huge streamliner car order that had been placed by C&O right after World War II wound up being sold to other railroads.

But a few railroads still believed in the future of the passenger train—notably Santa Fe, Union Pacific, Burlington, Seaboard, and Atlantic Coast Line—and continued buying new rolling stock into the 1960s. A few other roads reasoned that reinventing the streamliner in the 1950s could draw passengers back to the rails as it had in the 1930s. An early attempt to stem mounting losses was General Motors' ultra-lightweight *Aerotrain* of 1956, a string of Spartan, low center-of-gravity, aluminum bus bodies strung together behind a stainless-steel locomotive that looked like a wide-mouthed cousin of a 1950 Studebaker coupe. Though the Union Pacific and Pennsylvania gave the new equipment a tryout on regional routes, travelers rejected the *Aerotrain*'s rough-riding characteristics. Other low-slung trains of the era

employed a Spanish "Talgo" suspension, such as the Rock Island's *Jet Rocket*, New York Central's *Xplorer*, and the *Dan'l Webster* on the New Haven. But maintenance problems and passenger dissatisfaction soon led these back-to-the-future lightweights to a similar fate as the *Aerotrain*: demotion to commuter service and a premature trip to the scrap yard. With no panacea in sight for stemming the flow of red ink, and declining patronage permitting the retirement of most pre-World War II rolling stock, only a handful of railroads would purchase fewer than 100 new cars after 1958.

The design nadir continued well past May 1, 1971, when the U.S. government-formed quasi-public corporation Amtrak took over passenger-train operations on all railroads willing to pay an amount determined by their prior years' losses in either cash or equipment. The new national carrier had selected only the best of the disparate hand-me-downs, but the effect for on-board riders created more than a few schizophrenic train personalities: Indian-motif former *Super Chief* stainless-steel coaches arriving at Grand Central in

New York and a *California Zephyr* Vista-Dome sleeper-lounge observation car backing in to New Orleans' Union Passenger Terminal.

Surviving an initial era of political uncertainty with the knowledge that its aging cars and locomotives would soon need to be replaced, Amtrak began casting about for new ideas. Jet-engine technology provided the propulsion for United Aircraft's TurboTrain, which featured bright interiors and a dome lounge section at each end, the first self-contained trainset to do so. After a cross-country U. S. tour, the train entered service on the twisting, scenic shoreline route between Boston and New York. In the Midwest, two separate French Turboliner designs were tried out on routes radiating out of Chicago to Detroit, St. Louis, and Milwaukee beginning in 1973. But though the sparkling, large-windowed turbos were a

ABOVE: To update the look of the 1940s- and 1950s-era cars it inherited, Amtrak went "mod" in the 1970s with paisley fabrics and bright colors, graphically illustrated in this former Great Northern parlor observation car. Although borderline ghastly by contemporary standards, such impulsive graphics were then in vogue and helped bring passenger trains up to date—cosmetically anyway. MIKE SCHAFER

BELOW: A 1970s-era Budd-built Amfleet coach shortly after a refurbishment in the 1980s shows tasteful restraint, yet attractive color combinations. MIKE SCHAFER

welcome change from the rattletrap remnants of an earlier era, they proved unreliable. United Aircraft's prototype was shipped off to Canada. After being idled for over a decade, the French trains eventually were re-engined and refurbished with new interiors for use between New York City and Upstate New York destinations, where they would remain in service into the twenty-first century.

Instead of unique solutions dictated by regional requirements, Amtrak beginning in 1975 settled on "Amfleet" rolling stock—coaches and food-service cars that followed a stainless-steel tubular design rooted in the Budd Company's experimental, electric-powered *Metroliner* cars of 1966, built as part of a demonstration project for the U. S. Department of Transportation on Pennsylvania Railroad's New York–Washington route. The *Metroliner*s were the first U. S. trains to regularly achieve 125 MPH in revenue service.

Featuring a red-and-white stripe at window level outside and upholstered with red seats and brown rug walls inside in both high-density and long-distance versions, Amfleet

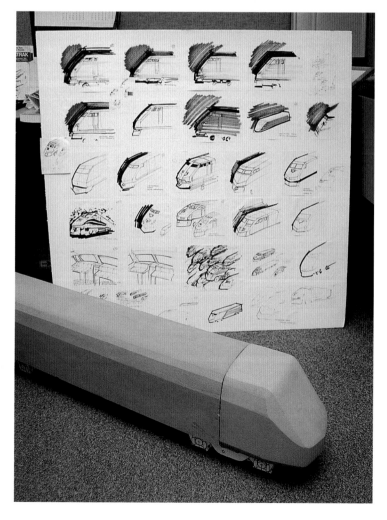

CESAR VERGARA

Industrial designer Cesar Vergara fine-tunes the nose design of Amtrak's then-yet-to-be-built General Electric "Genesis" passenger diesels. The finished product is shown on the previous page. Note the reference material by the keyboard. BOB JOHNSTON

Spanish-born designer Cesar Vergara remembers a class in Sweden in which the instructor asked his students to paint a cylinder two ways: going fast and standing still. It highlighted for him the interconnective role that paint and shape play in industrial design. When he had an opportunity to alter shapes of locomotives and passenger cars at Amtrak in the 1990s and today with the design firm of Walter Dorwin Teague & Associates, he grabbed it. "Successful streamlining utilizes bands of darkness and light that lead one's eye effortlessly from one part of the shape to the next. Interruptions lead to another shape, and you don't wonder where to look next," says Vergara. He contends that the biggest difference between designing now and in the 1930s and 1940s is the blessing and curse of the computer. "Shapes are tested for aerodynamic efficiency before a model is ever made. Back then, they created a beautiful shape first and may have tweaked it in wind tunnel tests." Vergara, who has put his mark on the shape and paint of the Genesis and FP59 locomotives as well as Amtrak's Talgo, sees today's higher-speed designs as a logical progression of what happened at the beginning of the streamliner era. "They are a link in the chain, but keep this in mind: there are about four links missing—caused by the moribund status of the U.S. passenger train from the mid-1950s to the mid 1990s." Fortunately, it seems, that era is now over.

would represent the Budd Company's last passenger-car order. In 1981, Pullman-Standard rang down its final curtain with a fleet of similarly bedecked bilevel Superliners—sleepers, glass-topped lounges, diners, and coaches, inspired by the aesthetic and operational success of Santa Fe's Hi-Level double-deckers that had been used on its *El Capitan, San Francisco Chief,* and *Texas Chief.*

By the early 1990s, when a second Superliner order began rolling out of French Canadian manufacturer Bombardier's U.S. factory at Barre, Vermont, and 50 single-level Viewliner sleeping cars replaced all but a handful of tired overnighters born just after World War II, Amtrak had begun taking passenger-train design more seriously. It had to. In 1990, auto-happy California passed a state bond issue that provided seed money to fund a statewide network of passenger trains voters hoped would take pressure off Golden State freeway traffic jams. Luring customers out of their cars with exciting new trains became a priority, just as it had 50-plus years earlier. But dwindling U.S. demand had decimated domestic manufacturing capability, so Amtrak had to design, build, and test Viewliner and "California Car" prototypes before it struck a deal with the only bidder, Morrison-Knudsen (later absorbed by Bombardier), which then had the workforce in place to build the initial order of California Cars. Using newly developed computer-based technology and input from focus groups and employees, both staff and consultant designers were able to efficiently test and implement elements as minute as lighted signage that glowed in a darkened sleeping-car room or as gargantuan as the shape and paint scheme of the General Electric "Genesis" and General Motors FP59 locomotives, which provided the crucial "first impression" for prospective passengers waiting on the platform.

Inspiration for much of the 1930s streamliner movement came from designers trained in Europe: both Henry Dreyfuss and Raymond Loewy were from France; Otto Kuhler hailed from Germany and Austria. Similarly, when Amtrak began looking for a "next generation of passenger trains" to excite the traveling public, it imported an off-the-shelf Swedish X2000 high-speed train, a German ICE train, and two Spanish Talgos for

ABOVE: Amtrak's Blair Slaughter displays his portfolio of interior car designs and fabrics for future new rolling stock. BOB JOHNSTON

BELOW: The interiors of Amtrak's new California Cars, developed jointly by Caltrans (California Department of Transportation) and Amtrak, rely heavily on high-impact plastic in the seating and overhead luggage racks. This coach is serving on the *San Joaquin* between Oakland and Bakersfield in 1996. BOB JOHNSTON

ABOVE: The Amtrak/Caltrans California Cars utilize the bilevel concept popularized by the Santa Fe in the 1950s. Because of the State of California's extended involvement in passenger train development and operation, state-sponsored trains often have their own paint scheme. BOB JOHNSTON

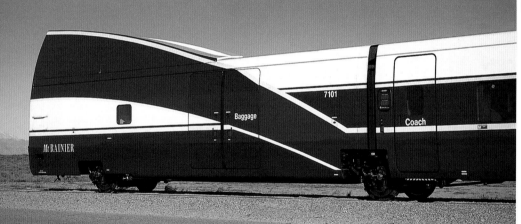

display and demonstration runs. The low-riding, articulated Talgo was too short for the high-level platforms found along the Boston–New York–Washington Northeast Corridor, but so impressed the Washington State Department of Transportation and Amtrak that they ordered a fleet of trains to be assembled by the Spanish company's American affiliate near Seattle. Placed in service in early 1999 as the *Cascades* between Eugene, Oregon, through Portland and Seattle to Vancouver, British Columbia, the green, cream, and brown speedsters sport twin six-foot fiberglass fins sweeping up from the window line on the end cars to the top of the back of the standard-issue FP59 locomotive so as to—in the words of European-trained Amtrak designer Cesar Vergara— "keep the train from looking like Chihuahuas following a St. Bernard." Inside, the design team crafted a painted ceiling of Puget Sound in the bistro car that features tiny lights representing towns. A "temperamental" shade of pink was deliberately chosen for the walls, which give the car a fresh look in daylight, but a warm glow when interacting with the recessed halogen lights at night.

Meanwhile, back in the Northeast Corridor, Amtrak would soon unveil *Acela Express* service, 150-MPH electric trainsets with power units at each end. Manufactured by a consortium of Bombardier and Alstom, builder of the French high-speed *TGV* trains that criss-cross France, the new American train features a café car with elliptical

One of the most striking examples of streamliner design since the days of Raymond Loewy, Henry Dreyfuss, and Otto Kuhler is the interior of the Bistro car of the Seattle-based Talgo trains operated by Amtrak and the State of Washington. Patrons sit around a semi-circular lunch counter or nearby booth seating, all under a ceiling map of the Puget Sound area, with pinpoints of light representing towns. BOB JOHNSTON

ABOVE LEFT AND RIGHT: Interiors of Amtrak's new high-speed *Acela Express* trains on the Boston–New York–Washington Northeast Corridor impart a spacious atmosphere. Bathrooms are completely handicapped-accessible and feature futuristic lighted mirrors. Galleys with cabinets for modular food storage permit efficient access to patrons in the first-class car. BOB JOHNSTON

BELOW: A twenty-first-century dining car? No, a 1958-vintage Budd-built former *North Coast Limited* dining car that Amtrak has refurbished. Pastels are back in vogue, fixed seating eliminates the tangle of individual chairs, and tables lift for easy accessibility. BOB JOHNSTON

tables and indirect lighting, stunning, circular-mirrored bathrooms that look as if they belong in a fine hotel, and a uniquely-rounded shape that is accented on both the front and sides of the train.

Both the *Cascades* and *Acela Express* are passenger-friendly, boasting tall, wide windows, comfortable foam seat cushions, and the latest at-seat technology and amenities of the day. Though each utilizes a different mechanical system, both employ a counter-balancing tilt when rounding curves, thereby minimizing discomfort resulting from centrifugal forces. And, like the very first streamliners—the M-10000 and *Zephyr* 9900—both are articulated trains with wheels positioned between the cars, which are permanently coupled. The main drawback inherent in articulation—lack of quickly being able to adjust train length to accommodate passenger demand—was to be offset by frequent schedules.

In a sense, then, the streamlined passenger train has come full-circle in this latest incarnation—ushering in a new era of high-speed travel in sleek, striking railcars. But don't weep for the last remnants of the post-World War II "modernization." Amtrak is completely refurbishing dining cars that once hosted passengers on the *North Coast Limited*, *Super Chief*, and *Denver Zephyr* with glass-etched booths, bright interior colors, and an open kitchen-lunch counter replacing the age-old arrangement of a dingy hallway next to an enclosed kitchen. And on the *American Orient Express*, a privately-operated luxury cruise train, sleepers from the B&O's *Capitol Limited*, lounges that used to be open-section sleepers on the *City of Los Angeles*, and a round-end observation car that once adorned the rear of the *20th Century Limited* still soldier on—now united in a train of perfectly matched blue and cream livery. In all its varied art forms, the streamlined era is still with us today.

LEFT AND BELOW: Although most post-World War II-era passenger cars have been scrapped, a few have been rescued by private entrepreneurs (and Amtrak) and refurbished for use in special train service. At left is the interior of the former New York Central sleeper-lounge observation car *Sandy Creek*, built for the 1948 *20th Century Limited*. The car is now known as the *New York* and—spectacularly renovated—serves on the *American-Orient Express* cruise train, shown below at Gaviota, California, in 1999. BOB JOHNSTON